Faithfully Formed

The Lutheran Confessions in Daily Life

ANDY WRIGHT

CONCORDIA PUBLISHING HOUSE · SAINT LOUIS

Published by Concordia Publishing House
3558 S. Jefferson Ave., St. Louis, MO 63118-3968
1-800-325-3040 • cph.org

Manufactured in the United States of America

Library of Congress Cataloging-in-Publication Data

Names: Wright, Andrew, 1985- author.

Title: Faithfully formed : the Lutheran confessions in daily life / Andy Wright.

Description: Saint Louis, MO : Concordia Publishing House, [2024] | Summary: "In the book, the author presents a clear perspective on how the Lutheran Confessions address essential questions in the lives of people today. He uses Christ-centered language to integrate critical Confessional doctrine with contemporary issues"-- Provided by publisher.

Identifiers: LCCN 2024000103 (print) | LCCN 2024000104 (ebook) | ISBN 9780758673954 (paperback) | ISBN 9780758673961 (ebook)

Subjects: LCSH: Lutheran Church--Creeds.

Classification: LCC BX8068.A1 W75 2024 (print) | LCC BX8068.A1 (ebook) | DDC 238/.41--dc23/eng/20240226

LC record available at https://lccn.loc.gov/2024000103

LC ebook record available at https://lccn.loc.gov/2024000104

---

1 2 3 4 5 6 7 8 9 10 33 32 31 30 29 28 27 26 25 24

PRAISE FOR *FAITHFULLY FORMED*

Pastor Andy Wright poses three fundamental questions—regarding God's identity, what it means to be human, and how we relate to God's creation—as the framework for setting forth the testimony of the Book of Concord that defines the Lutheran confession of faith in Christ and proclamation of the message of Scripture. This volume takes readers into the text of the Lutheran confessional documents and engages the foundations of our trust in the Creator; the restoration of our humanity through the incarnation, death, and resurrection of Christ; and the work of delivering absolution and new life of the Holy Spirit. Wright's guide to exploration of the historical confessions effectively stimulates individual readers and study groups to absorb the confessions' content into their own way of thinking.

—Robert Kolb, emeritus professor of systematic theology,
Concordia Seminary, St. Louis

To the lay reader, Pastor Wright has given an inviting—and highly teachable—introduction to the documents that make us Lutheran Christians. To the pastor, he's given a thoughtful review in which we'll each still discover new gems. To both, he's given a reading of the confessions and a hearing of Christ that puts them in the context of life—as perhaps has never been done quite this way before.

—Dr. Carl C. Fickenscher II, professor of pastoral ministry
and missions, Concordia Theological Seminary,
Fort Wayne, Indiana

The Lutheran Confessions are a tremendous gift for us all. *Faithfully Formed* connects the Lutheran Confessions to everyday life and ordinary questions. Pastor Wright has authored a wonderful resource for living out our confessional heritage. I am excited to use this book within my congregation!

—Rev. Dr. A. Trevor Sutton, senior pastor,
St. Luke Lutheran Church; author of *Being Lutheran*

TABLE OF CONTENTS

ABBREVIATIONS

AC	Augsburg Confession
Ap	Apology of the Augsburg Confession
FC	Formula of Concord
FC Ep	Epitome of the Formula of Concord
FC SD	Solid Declaration of the Formula of Concord
LC	Large Catechism of Martin Luther
SA	Smalcald Articles
SC	Small Catechism of Martin Luther
Tr	Treatise on the Power and Primacy of the Pope

CITATION EXAMPLES

AC XX 4 (Augsburg Confession, Article XX, paragraph 4)

Ap IV 229 (Apology of the Augsburg Confession, Article IV, paragraph 229)

FC Ep V 8 (Epitome of the Formula of Concord, Article V, paragraph 8)

FC SD X 24 (Solid Declaration of the Formula of Concord, Article X, paragraph 24)

LC V 32, 37 (Large Catechism, Part 5, paragraphs 32 and 37)

SA III I 6 (Smalcald Articles, Part III, Article I, paragraph 6)

SC III 5 (Small Catechism, Part III, paragraph 5)

Tr 5 (Treatise, paragraph 5)

PREFACE

This book aims to show and help Christians see how they are formed by God's Word as confessed in the Lutheran Confessions. The Book of Concord is practical and speaks to our daily lives as we live in faith toward God and in love toward our neighbors. It helps us confess Christ and see how we think, speak, and act as the baptized children of God. It calls us to repentance as it preaches that we have failed to be conformed to the Word of God and sinned against Him in our various walks of life. It also teaches and shows the path God would have us walk as His people who have been bought with His own blood. Above all, it gives us Jesus as pastors preach to us how God has forgiven our sins on account of Christ and how we now stand righteous before the throne of God.

This book has come about from numerous Bible studies, discussions, papers, lectures, and sermons as well as the overall pastoral care of God's people. Time and again, it never ceases to amaze me how practical the Lutheran Confessions are in the lives of God's people. I will forever remember serving a congregation in Iowa and meeting on Thursday mornings at 6:30 for a men's Bible study. We had previously studied various books of the Bible and did a study on the Reformation. This led to some questions from the group about the Lutheran Confessions, so I very eagerly encouraged us to go through the Book of Concord.

There were a few grumbles at the beginning of the study. Finally, one morning we were reading and discussing the article concerning confession in the Smalcald Articles. One of the men, a retired farmer who had been on board with the study in theory but hadn't yet seen any real practical use for it, made a comment about how confession got him thinking about Christ and the Gospel. The article on confession in the Smalcald Articles, something he had never ever heard or thought of before, turned on a light bulb that helped him connect the dots to understand more about the Gospel. It formed how he looked at the means of grace and prompted him to encourage his children and grandchildren with the Gospel.

That incident is not an isolated one. I've been a pastor for a little over a decade now and have used the Lutheran Confessions in so many ways and circumstances. I've used them rejoicing with a couple preparing for marriage. I've used the Lutheran Confessions and Christ's gifts with a mother who just lost her child. I've used them as a father with my own children. I've used them to help teach future pastors on another continent. The list goes on, but the Lutheran Confessions are the same. They have formed me to think confessionally.

I love the Lutheran Confessions because they teach and preach Christ and His Word. Above all, they confess the Scriptures. They form and shape us, as they have been normed and formed by the Word of God, and we confess these documents with the whole church through the ages. We confess this same faith as the apostles, countless church fathers, saints, martyrs, Martin Luther, Martin Chemnitz, Johann Gerhard, C. F. W. Walther, and saints in Iowa and Kansas. Think about it. This great treasure we have in these documents is good, true, and beautiful to read, study, and confess.

Introduction

Christians think differently and look at the world differently. That doesn't mean we stand on our heads or walk backward down the street. It means that because we are in Christ and have His Word, we think differently than the fallen world around us. God, through Paul, writes in Romans 12:1–2, "I appeal to you therefore, brothers, by the mercies of God, to present your bodies as a living sacrifice, holy and acceptable to God, which is your spiritual worship. Do not be conformed to this world, but be transformed by the renewal of your mind, that by testing you may discern what is the will of God, what is good and acceptable and perfect."

Perhaps you have heard these verses before or even read and come back to them often. Regardless, we hear through these words that God calls us to present our lives as living sacrifices. This is done as we live in faith toward God and in love toward our neighbors. This means not conforming to the world but being transformed by the renewal of our minds. The Greek word here is related to the word "metamorphosis" that is used when a caterpillar changes into a butterfly. Now God is not saying we change from being a man or woman into a frog or a butterfly. No, He teaches us that as baptized children of God, we are new creations. We have been crucified with Christ, and there are real ramifications for our lives even now. The world around us isn't supposed to form how we think, speak, and act. Our minds instead have been renewed by the Holy Spirit, and how we think, speak, and act is formed and conformed to the Word of God, the Holy Scriptures.

The Lutheran Confessions understand this as they confess the Scriptures. As Lutherans, we often get asked, "What is the relationship between the Scriptures and the Lutheran Confessions?" As people who teach *sola Scriptura* (or Scripture alone), where do the Lutheran Confessions fit into this? Isn't God's Word, well, enough? Some drive a wedge between these two biblical concepts—Scriptures and confessing the faith. They may say, "I don't have any creeds. I have the Bible." How should we respond?

Scriptures and the Lutheran Confessions are not opposed to each other. The Word of God creates the confession and provides the substance of the Lutheran Confessions. The fruit this confession produces, which has been formed by the Word of God, is the confession of that same thing that brought it about. For example, the Gospel produces faith, and faith confesses the Gospel. In Matthew 16:13–19, we read that flesh and blood did not reveal Jesus as the Christ to Peter; it was the Father in heaven. What Peter said is what the Scriptures had testified to him about Jesus. His confession is an answer back in faith.

One often sees two terms used in theology when studying the relationship between the Holy Scriptures and the Lutheran Confessions. These are *norma normans* and *norma normata*. *Norma normans* means "the ruling rule" or the "norming norm," which refers to the Bible as that which determines doctrine.

The Lutheran Confessions speak about the Holy Scriptures in this way in numerous places, with the beginning of the Formula of Concord being one of the most well known. It states, "First, <we receive and embrace with our whole heart> are the prophetic and apostolic Scriptures of the Old and New Testaments as the pure, clear fountain of Israel. They are the only true standard or norm by which all teachers and doctrines are to be judged."[1] Scripture "norms" all teaching, teachers, and practices in the church because it alone

1 FC SD Summary 3.

is God's Word. This means that everything we believe, teach, and confess comes only from the Scriptures.

The second, *norma normata*, means the "ruled rule" or the "normed norm." In this way, there is a measure by which teachers and practices in the church are judged if they are faithfully teaching what the Scriptures teach. An example of this can be seen in the doctrine of Holy Baptism. What Baptism is and everything it entails is taught in the Bible. When a document in the Lutheran Confessions (like the Small Catechism) teaches about Baptism, it confesses, or says back, what the Scriptures reveal Baptism is, what Baptism gives, and what Baptism means for our lives. The same goes for other topics and themes. All these confessional documents, though, give a public witness of what we believe the Scriptures teach. They are used to compare teachings and teachers in a similar way to the Scriptures so that when you encounter a teaching on Baptism, if it is line with the Small Catechism or the Augsburg Confession, then you know this is what the Scriptures teach since the Lutheran Confessions are faithful witnesses of the Scriptures.

Doctrine is practical. The Lutheran Confessions show this well as we think about confessing the faith to one another in our homes, churches, schools, jobs, communities, and anywhere else God has placed us. The Lutheran Confessions organize and summarize the truths of God's Word in ways in which we can study and discuss with one another and give answer to the world around us. Questions like "Who is God?" can be answered with "I believe in God the Father Almighty, maker of heaven and earth . . ." We give answer based on what God has revealed to us about who He is in the Bible and the Creeds. These foundational sources form and aid what we confess.

We are not alone in our answer. The Lutheran Confessions unfurl the flag, so to speak, and identify us as those who believe what we do about justification, the church, and everything else. What does a Lutheran believe about the church? The Lutheran Confessions answer this by asking a similar question: What does the Bible teach about the church? What the Lutheran Confessions teach is what the Scriptures teach because they are normed by the Scriptures themselves.

The Lutheran Confessions are nothing apart from the Word of God. With God's Word, however, they are a great treasure of the church that speaks the Christian faith in this world. Just as the Holy Scriptures are relevant for our lives, so are the Lutheran Confessions. While we might not be engaged in the same discussions or controversies as some of the writers of the various documents, the truth of what is written still shines through presently. When Peter said to Jesus, "You are the Christ, the Son of living God" (Matthew 16:16), there was no time stamp on that; it is the rock of the church that will never crumble or decay. That same clear confession is made today by the church of Christ and each of us as individual members of that Body.

The Lutheran Confessions are used and confessed in our lives. They are not simply documents mentioned in our church constitutions or documents we studied in seminary and then never used in our lives. The Lutheran Confessions help us think confessionally as we look at our lives and our confession of Christ. We use them in ways that help us "think about" (to borrow a phrase used in the Formula of Concord) issues, concepts, and various other aspects we face as the baptized people of God. We think about and confess the Lutheran Confessions, which is to say we are thinking about and confessing the Holy Scriptures. This is the confidence we have in God's Word.

It is with that confidence that we join with the signers of the Formula of Concord in understanding what it means to have God's Word and give answer before God and the world:

In the sight of God and of all Christendom <the entire Church of Christ>, we want to testify to those now living and those who will come after us. This declaration presented here about all the controverted articles mentioned and explained above—and

no other—is our faith, doctrine, and confession. By God's grace, with intrepid hearts, we are willing to appear before the judgment seat of Christ with this Confession and give an account of it [1 Peter 4:5]. We will not speak or write anything contrary to this Confession, either publicly or privately. By the strength of God's grace we intend to abide by it.[2]

2 FC SD XII 40.

Introduction and Summaries to the Documents of the Book of Concord

CONCORDIA: *THE LUTHERAN CONFESSIONS*

Note: *The following few pages are a simple review of contents of the Book of Concord. If you are already familiar with these, feel free to skip ahead to Section I.*

The Lutheran Confessions are documents that confess the Holy Scriptures. These various texts are contained in the Book of Concord. It is also known as Concordia, as the title page of the Book of Concord, published in 1580, has the word *Concordia* written in red above all the other text. The word *Concordia* comes from a word meaning harmony or unity. That's an important thing that tells us the purpose of these documents. They are unified and confess the truth of the Scriptures in the past, the present, and future.

The Three Ecumenical Creeds

The three Universal or Ecumenical Creeds of the Christian Church make up the first document in the Lutheran Confessions. Creeds are formal statements of what one believes. Because the faith confessed in the Lutheran Confessions is nothing new, the Three

Ecumenical Creeds are placed first. The Ecumenical Creeds clarify the faith confessed in the Scriptures and passed down through the ages beginning with the apostles.

The Ecumenical Creeds are the Apostles', the Nicene, and the Athanasian. The oldest of these is the Apostles' Creed, which dates back to the second century. It is a baptismal creed (or statement of faith made during Baptisms). The second, as we know its form today, is the Nicene Creed. It comes out the affirmations of the Scriptures of two councils that addressed false teachings about Jesus and the Trinity. Those two councils were the Councils of Nicaea, held in 325, and Constantinople, held in 381. Lastly, the Athanasian Creed dates to sometime between the sixth and eighth centuries. Athanasius did not write the text, but it is named after him. Athanasius was at the Council of Nicaea and defended the doctrine of the Holy Trinity against false teachings.

The Augsburg Confession

Sometimes called the Magna Carta of the Lutheran Church, the Augsburg Confession was written by Philip Melanchthon, a close colleague of Luther in Wittenberg. Various other documents by Melanchthon were incorporated into this confession. It is common for the Lutheran Church to be referred to as the church of the Augsburg Confession. This is true in some of the documents in the Lutheran Confessions. The Augsburg Confession is broken into two parts. The first part, Articles I–XXI, address the chief articles of the faith. The second part, Articles XXII–XXVIII, addresses many of the specific abuses that occurred within the Roman Catholic Church. Even with these two parts, the whole of the Augsburg Confession comes back to and stems out of Article IV, "Justification."

This confession of faith was presented to Holy Roman Emperor Charles V at a diet (imperial meeting) in Augsburg on June 25, 1530. It was presented by Melanchthon along with various princes as they answered what the true faith is and what was being taught and confessed by the pastors and people in their regions.

The Apology of the Augsburg Confession

The Apology is a response to the response of papal or Roman theologians in a document called the Confutation. The Apology was also written by Melanchthon and published in 1531. It defends what the Augsburg Confession states and takes a more in-depth look at some of the articles as it addresses the implications of various theological topics and assertations. It serves the church well to see how the confession made at Augsburg the year prior was nothing new. The Apology helps the church proclaim Christ and His Word faithfully and console God's people.

The Smalcald Articles

As the Reformation was in full swing, the reformers kept open the possibility of a future council to discuss the issues at hand between the churches of the Reformation and the Roman Catholic Church. Luther wrote the Smalcald Articles at the end of 1536 at the request of his ruler, John Frederick. The articles were intended to be discussed at a theological conference of theologians and lay leaders at Smalcald, Germany. These articles were never used as originally envisioned, however. Instead, Luther used them as an opportunity to confess the faith clearly and boldly after he had suffered a significant illness.

The Smalcald Articles are divided into three parts. The first part deals with a confession of who God is and is a summary of the Ecumenical Creeds, which confess the Holy Trinity. The second part deals with our redemption in Christ and includes articles that address the abuse of the doctrine of justification by grace through faith in Christ alone, such as the sacrifice of the mass and the papacy. The third and final part contains articles to be discussed, which really is to say to be confessed over and above errors that have arisen.

Treatise on the Power and Primacy of the Pope

This document was the third in the Lutheran Confessions written by Melanchthon. Along with some of the background to the

Smalcald Articles, this document, which was written in 1537, was to be attached to the Augsburg Confession to clarify Lutherans' understanding of the papacy. Sometimes, though, this document is seen as an addendum to the Smalcald Articles.

The purpose of this document is to clearly lay out the erroneous teachings regarding the papacy and the impact these have on other articles of the faith, such as the office of the ministry, the church, and, most especially, salvation. Addressing the claims of the papacy and what this means, this document rightly points to how the doctrine of the papacy has the marks of the antichrist.

The Small and Large Catechisms

Serving as a visitor at various churches in Saxony, Luther observed the need to teach the faith to families. Pastors were also in dire need of catechesis so that they could remain students of God's Word and the doctrine it teaches. Luther began preaching three series of sermons, each varying in number, on the catechism (the Ten Commandments, the Creed, and the Lord's Prayer, which were the primary texts of catechisms at the time) in 1528. The final ten sermons on the catechism were preached in November and December 1528 and served to form much of the basis and content of what became the Large Catechism.

In 1529, the Large and Small Catechisms were published. The Large Catechism was published before the Small Catechism and has a very distinct sermon sound and tone to it. It is intended to aid pastors and fathers as they teach the faith to God's people. The Small Catechism was published as a handbook of the Christian faith for fathers to teach their households the things of God as they are summarized in the Six Chief Parts.

As a note, throughout history, some other documents have been attached to various editions of the Large and Small Catechisms and the Book of Concord. Some examples include "A Marriage Booklet for Simple Pastors" and "The Baptismal Booklet." These were included at the end of some editions of the Small Catechism.

"A Brief Exhortation to Confession" was included in a revised edition of the Large Catechism in 1529 but was not included in the 1580 edition of the Book of Concord.

The Formula of Concord, Epitome and Solid Declaration

The final document in the Lutheran Confessions, the Formula of Concord, has two parts. The Epitome is the shorter, abridged version of the longer Solid Declaration. These were written as one document in 1577. Several authors such as Chemnitz, Nicholas Selnecker, Jacob Andreae, David Chytraeus, Christopher Cornerus, and Andrew Musculus contributed to this document along with several other writers. The Formula of Concord addressed many issues that arose in the Lutheran Church both from within and outside, such as Calvinism. The Formula of Concord continues the confession of faith already made in the previous documents of the Lutheran Confessions as it seeks to make this bold and faithful confession amid new and reoccurring controversies.

At first glance, the Formula of Concord, especially the Solid Declaration, may appear to be a lofty theological treatise. While this is the case, the concern is for the proclamation of Christ, the consolation of God's people, the church, and the unity or Concord they have in the Scriptures. This is the unity found in the doctrine they believe, teach, and confess.

A Catalog of Testimonies

This list of references and quotes was appended to many early editions of the Book of Concord. This catalog was included to show and reaffirm that Formula of Concord's confession of the person of Christ was not anything new and, in fact, was in harmony with the orthodox faith throughout church history.

NAME	DATE	AUTHOR	SUMMARY
Apostles' Creed	Second Century	Unknown	Baptismal creed used in Rome.
Nicene Creed	325, 381	Assembled church leaders at the Council of Nicaea (325) and the Council of Constantinople (381)	Creed intended to clearly state, on the basis of Scripture, that Jesus Christ is true God, equal with the Father, and that the Holy Spirit is also true God, equal with the Father and the Son.
Athanasian Creed	Sixth–Eighth Centuries	Unknown; named after the great church father Athanasius, who was instrumental in the drafting of the Nicene Creed	Confession of the teaching of the Trinity and the person and work of Jesus Christ.
Small Catechism	1529	Martin Luther	A short work that was to educate the laity in the basics of the Christian faith.
Large Catechism	1529	Martin Luther	A series of re-edited sermons of Luther that cover the same chief parts of Christian doctrine as the Small Catechism.
Augsburg Confession	June 25, 1530	Philip Melanchthon	The chief Lutheran Confession, which was presented by the earliest Lutherans to Emperor Charles V at the Imperial Diet of Augsburg as a statement of the chief articles of the Christian faith as understood by Lutherans; also contains a listing of abuses that the Lutherans had corrected.

NAME	DATE	AUTHOR	SUMMARY
Apology of the Augsburg Confession	May 1531	Philip Melanchthon	A lengthy defense authored by Melanchthon after the Roman theologians had condemned many of the teachings of the Augsburg Confession; rightly considered a Christian classic.
Smalcald Articles	1536	Martin Luther	Articles of faith intended by Luther to be an ecumenical platform for an upcoming church council; stated what the Lutherans could not compromise and why.
Treatise on the Power and Primacy of the Pope	1537	Philip Melanchthon	A supplement to the Augsburg Confession that gives the Lutheran position on the pope.
Formula of Concord	1577	Jacob Andreae, Martin Chemnitz, Nicholas Selnecker	A restatement of some teachings in the Augsburg Confession over which Lutherans had become divided. The Solid Declaration is the unabridged version. The Epitome is an abridged version intended for congregations to study. More than 8,100 pastors and theologians signed it, as well as more than 50 government leaders.

SECTION I

Who Is God?

Why is it important to not only believe in God but to know who He is?

It's often said that the two topics you don't talk about with people are religion and politics. The reason given is because everyone seems to have his own thoughts on the matter. We are taught, too, either directly or indirectly, that religion and the things of God are personal or private matters. God, though, shows us something about Himself in all of this, including how easily we can try to create our own gods (even if we don't realize this is happening).

There is only one true God, the Holy Trinity. God is knowable as He reveals Himself. He is not simply some deity in the sky but personal, and He knows us personally. Our confession about God rests on who He tells us He is according to His Word. Seeing God revealed to us in the Scriptures means we see our God, who has redeemed us in Christ and is still at work in our lives through the means of grace.

CHAPTER 1

Do We Know Who God Is?

The Father, Son, and Holy Spirit, three distinct persons in one divine essence and nature [Matthew 28:19], are one God, who has created heaven and earth [1 Corinthians 8:6].[3]

As I began writing this, it was the festival of St. Peter and St. Paul in the Church Year. The Holy Gospel appointed for this day is Matthew 16:13–19. In that reading, Jesus asks the question, "Who do people say that the Son of Man is?" (v. 13). After the disciples give Him some answers, Jesus asks them, "But who do you say that I am?" (v. 14).

That's quite a question, isn't? Really, though, this is the question all of us are asked as we bear the name of Christ in this world as His people. God's Word speaks and gives us both the content and the faith to confess Christ. It's really nothing short of a miracle that this happens. It's also a wonderful blessing in our lives to have this confession placed upon our lips. The Christian faith is not some abstract philosophical concept. The Christian faith is knowable and personal. That gets, then, to the answer of Peter in Matthew 16:

3 SA Preface The First Part.

"Simon Peter replied, 'You are the Christ, the Son of the living God'" (v. 16). Jesus is God in the flesh. He is the Son of God.

This confession of Christ has been made by Christians throughout history and continues throughout the world. We don't stand alone in our confession of Christ. As we think about what God has given to us and revealed about Himself through the Scriptures, we see the Three Ecumenical Creeds confess what the Scriptures teach. This is where the Ecumenical Creeds and their explanations are helpful for us not only in understanding who God is but in how we speak about God in our lives and confess Him in various situations.

There is a reason why the Book of Concord begins with the Three Ecumenical Creeds. They lay out what God clearly teaches in His Word about who He is and what He has done in Christ. This is what has been said about Him for centuries and up to now. The Scriptures have not changed, so our confession of what the Scriptures teach does not change. In this unchanging biblical confession, we are joining with company that goes back 500; 1,700; and 2,000 years!

The Ecumenical Creeds also help us as we go about our lives confessing Christ. They shape how we speak about God and how we know and make distinctions about who God is and is not. One of the misnomers about the Creeds is that when they were written, people devised new teachings about God. For example, some people today claim that until the Council of Nicaea in 325, no one had ever thought of Jesus and the Father being one God. Some claim the Council decided to "make" Him God. No, that's not the case. What is said and confessed in the Creed(s) about Jesus is made clear in the Scriptures. These three Creeds—the Apostles', the Nicene, and the Athanasian—are simply confessing or mirroring what the Scriptures teach. They are doing this as they also reject false teachings contrary to the Scriptures.

The Lutheran Confessions also show us how Scripture is clear. The Bible contains many things that are hard to understand, to be sure, but that does not negate the fact that what the Scriptures teach are clear. The Lutheran Confessions show how Christians of different times, locations, and languages can confess the faith in the same way because of the clear content of the Scriptures.

The divine authorship of the Scriptures is paramount to understanding and forming the confession of the Christian faith. Apart from this inspiration of God, there is neither reliability nor need for concerning oneself with the Bible, either as the only source of what it means to confess the faith or for the content of this confession. Likewise, if there are any errors in the revealed Scriptures, any confession of that Word of God would be subject to scrutiny.

If God's Word is clear, then a clear confession is possible, and one can confess truth over and above error. If there is ambiguity in God's Word, then confession would, in turn, be impossible. Peter would have had to answer Jesus' question in Matthew 16 differently: "Well, it is not really clear who You are, so who am I to say what is right?" The clarity of the Word of God and the confession of the faith are important.

In some ways, then, there is a sort of principle the Creeds lay out when it comes to confessing Christ. This recurs throughout the Lutheran Confessions. One theologian once wrote that the Lutheran "regards confessional statements as a systematized compilation of Biblical principles of faith, the decisional premises for life, rather than a restrictive straitjacket. The anticonfessional Christian seeks the broadest base for agreement and cannot understand the need for delineating doctrine in clear detail."[4] We confess the truth and reject what is false. That may seem like an obvious point, but really, something very important forms our thinking. By contrast, neither delineating truth from error nor making a clear confession of faith is restrictive. There is something very freeing with the Lutheran Confessions, as they don't subject us to the whims and ways of the day or the loudest voice and personality of the time. Confessing faithfully who God is and what His Word says gives us the freedom

4 Robert D. Preus and Wilbert H. Rosin, eds., *A Contemporary Look at the Formula of Concord* (St. Louis: Concordia Publishing House, 1978), 93.

to always speak the truth in all places. Underpinning all of this is the clarity of Scriptures and the fact that the author is none other than God Himself.

God reveals Himself, and we confess Him. In a broad sense, we acknowledge that God is not one option among many. There is only one God. Likewise, Jesus says in John 14:6, "I am the way, and the truth, and the life. No one comes to the Father except through Me." Likewise, in Acts 4:11–12, God teaches, "This Jesus is the stone that was rejected by you, the builders, which has become the cornerstone. And there is salvation in no one else, for there is no other name under heaven given among men by which we must be saved."

The temptation to want to seek a god or a religion apart from the one true God is real. There are plenty of false teachings in the world around us that want us to conform to false beliefs and ways of life. Every day, a new in vogue mindset is crying out, seeking to be the loudest voice and gain headway in the hearts and minds of people. Even the saying "I am spiritual but not religious," which is a few years old now, is alive and well. All these mindsets tempt us to place man at the center of the universe and seek to claim a false virtue to somehow place themselves above the Christian faith.

The devil, the world, and our fallen flesh want a god who is moldable on the one hand and unknowable on the other. If our spirituality can define who God is, then we don't have to worry about how we think about God or what we say about Him. In this mindset, we are in the driver's seat, and God is whoever I want Him to be.

This is nothing new though, and it shouldn't surprise us. The Smalcald Articles confess something that helps us see the danger around us and calls us back to where we should find God in our lives:

All this is the old devil and old serpent [Revelation 12:9], who also turned Adam and Eve into enthusiasts. He led them away from God's outward Word to spiritualizing and self-pride [Genesis 3:2–5]. And

yet, he did this through other outward words. In the same way, our enthusiasts today condemn the outward Word. Yet they themselves are not silent. They fill the world with their babbling and writings, as if the Spirit could not come through the apostles' writings and spoken Word, but has to come through their writings and words. Why don't they leave out their own sermons and writings and let the Spirit Himself come to people without their writings before them, as they boast that He has come into them without the preaching of the Scriptures? We do not have time now to argue about this in more detail. We have treated this well enough elsewhere.[5]

The devil knows that God is real and that He speaks truth. The devil also knows how God reveals Himself to us and works in our lives. From the very fall into sin, Satan went after the Word of God and tried to spiritualize things for us humans and disconnect God from His Word. Take away the Word of God, and you take away not only how we know God but how He has promised to work and give us His gifts in Christ.

In this way, God does not leave us searching but speaks. His Word speaks to us even now as we go through this life, and we do not have to wonder, *Did God really say that?* For the Holy Scriptures tell us what God has really said. The devil wants obscurity and ambiguity, whereas the Scriptures and the confession of them are clear and precise.

When questions arise about what we believe, God calls us to confess Him. We do so as people known personally by God and who confess Him in a very personal way. When we confess Jesus and what He has done, we do so as a people who belong to Him. This forms not only how we confess Jesus but what we say about Him.

5 SA III VIII 5–6.

Christianity confesses. A popular opinion, however, is the idea that Christianity can be confession-less. Yet go back to that passage from Matthew 16. Jesus asks, "Who do you say that I am?" Peter's response, "You are the Christ," is a creedal statement. He makes a confession of who Jesus is, which says something about Jesus' person and work.

Think about when someone says, "I believe in Jesus." This is an essential confession. Yet when we ask further questions like "What does this mean?"; "Who is Jesus?"; "Why do you need Jesus?"; "What does He save you from?"; and "How do you have salvation?" the answers to those questions confess something particular. The only way one can rightly know the answer to who Jesus is is to look at what the Bible teaches. The Father in heaven reveals to Peter that Jesus is the Christ, the Son of the living God, and when Peter speaks, he confesses this answer to Jesus. Peter confesses the faith, and even in these few words, he speaks a creed.

Another point to this confession of God is what He does. Just as we want to mold God into our image and likeness, we also want to turn Jesus into a false Christ. Maybe this false Christ exists just to be our moral teacher or to make us feel all warm and fuzzy. While there may be aspects of who Jesus is in those descriptions, the Scriptures reveal Him to be something so much greater.

Thinking about all this can be confusing. Luther's explanation of the Second Article of the Apostles' Creed in the Small Catechism offers a wonderful, true confession of who Jesus is and what He has done for us:

I believe that Jesus Christ, true God, begotten of the Father from eternity, and also true man, born of the Virgin Mary, is my Lord. He has redeemed me, a lost and condemned creature, purchased and won me from all sins, from death, and from the power of the devil. He did this not with gold or silver, but with His

holy, precious blood and with His innocent suffering and death, so that I may be His own, live under Him in His kingdom, and serve Him in everlasting righteousness, innocence, and blessedness, just as He is risen from the dead, lives and reigns to all eternity. This is most certainly true.[6]

To know and confess who God is and that Jesus is "my Lord" who has "has redeemed me" is to confess God, who has saved us by His own blood. In the explanation of the Second Article, Luther draws upon the language of Scripture, showing us how we are to think about and confess Jesus. This confession is more than in a god who is unknowable, whose ways and works are unclear, and it's more than confessing a god who just came to be a good teacher or provide a nice sentiment in our lives. No, we confess that Jesus came to redeems us.

The Christian faith is personal, just as God is personal and not some nebulous spirit in the sky. We are set apart as the people of God not only in what we say but who we are in this world. The church is different, and Christians are different in our thinking, speaking, and living in this world.

God is not whoever I want Him to be. The Scriptures show us this, and the Lutheran Confessions help us confess it. To know this truth about God, in turn, forms our view of the world around us and how we interact with it. The Lutheran Confessions guide us to see that God, the true God, has created all things; He is the same one who commands us, "You shall have no other gods" (Exodus 20:3; Deuteronomy 5:7).

God calls us to examine our lives as we read and hear His Word and know who He is and who we are before Him. In some ways, this formation of our thinking as Christians begins with us dying to ourselves and to the world. It causes us to ask tough questions and, as

6 SC II.

Luther preaches in the Large Catechism, "Let everyone, then, see to it that he values this commandment great and high above all things. Do not regard it as a joke! Ask and examine your heart diligently [2 Corinthians 13:5], and you will find out whether it clings to God alone or not. . . . If, on the contrary, your heart clings to anything else from which it expects more good and help than from God, and if your heart does not take refuge in Him but flees from Him when in trouble, then you have an idol, another god."[7]

Confessing God is something we can't do on our own. The ability to confess God rightly is truly a gift from Him that He gives us through His Word. It forms our confession of what we say as we give answer to the question "Who do you say that I am?" We are clear in our confession as we speak the Scriptures, and we stand with the church throughout the ages in this same confession and faith that has been handed down to us. We treasure things like the Creeds and the Book of Concord as they shape and form our confession of who God is and what this means for us and the world both now and into eternity.

QUESTIONS FOR FURTHER DISCUSSION AND STUDY:

1. Read the Three Ecumenical Creeds at the beginning of the Book of Concord. What do each of these Creeds say in similar ways about God? How do each of these Creeds add further clarifications?

2. How do the Large and Small Catechisms connect each person of the Trinity with specific work? How does this help form how we think and speak about God?

7 LC I 28.

CHAPTER 2

Is Everything Really about Jesus?

Our churches teach that the Word, that is, the Son of God [John 1:14], *assumed the human nature in the womb of the Blessed Virgin Mary. So there are two natures—the divine and the human—inseparably joined in one person. There is one Christ, true God and true man, who was born of the Virgin Mary, truly suffered, was crucified, died, and was buried. He did this to reconcile the Father to us and to be a sacrifice, not only for original guilt, but also for all actual sins of mankind* [John 1:29].

He also descended into hell, and truly rose again on the third day. Afterward, He ascended into heaven to sit at the right hand of the Father. There He forever reigns and has dominion over all creatures. He sanctifies those who believe in Him, by sending the Holy Spirit into their hearts to rule, comfort, and make them alive. He defends them against the devil and the power of sin.

The same Christ will openly come again to judge the living and the dead, and so forth, according to the Apostles' Creed.[8]

8 AC III 1–6.

Why is everything about Jesus? That's a question that sounds a bit odd to ask, especially for those of us who have grown up in the Christian faith. It is, however, not always obvious to everyone and gets asked by people wanting to know why Christians talk about Jesus so much.

I vividly remember sitting at a winkel (a monthly pastor gathering) at a sister congregation, and one of my brother pastors told the story of an adult who was preparing to be confirmed and was finishing her time of adult instruction. The pastor recounted how the woman said she had one question for him. As a side note, when a pastor usually hears something like this (and in this tone), it is usually not going to be a pleasant question. Her question was, "I was at a funeral in a Lutheran Church recently, and all the pastor talked about was Jesus. Why didn't he make this person's funeral sermon not about her but about Jesus?" At this question, the brother pastor sighed a sigh of relief and told her why he made everything in the funeral about Jesus.

The reason is because Jesus is our salvation. The only hope we have in death is found in the Lord, who alone has died for us to atone for our sin. He is the resurrection and the life. For those who die in the Christian faith, this is our confidence, our consolation, and our peace. Preaching Christ, hearing about Christ, and singing about Christ at a funeral means having life amid death.

That gets to something so important that it cannot be stressed enough. Everything about God points us to Jesus; it really does. Everything in Christians' lives point us to who Christ is and what this means for us now and into eternity. Christ is our redemption. We are justified in the sight of God solely on account of Christ. The doctrine of justification is the doctrine of the Christian faith upon which the church stands or falls. In the Smalcald Articles, Luther calls justification the "chief article." He confesses,

The first and chief article is this:

Jesus Christ, our God and Lord, died for our sins and was raised again for our justification (Romans 4:24–25). . . .

Upon this article everything that we teach and practice depends, in opposition to the pope, the devil, and the whole world. Therefore, we must be certain and not doubt this doctrine. Otherwise, all is lost, and the pope, the devil, and all adversaries win the victory and the right over us.[9]

The Lutheran Confessions form how we think about Christ and what He has done. Everything points to Him and His work and to the fact we are justified by grace alone and through faith in Christ alone. The Small and Large Catechisms bring this all to a head and form us when they confess that Jesus is "my Lord."

The Large Catechism confesses Christ in a way that helps us think and confess who Christ is for us and for the world. Luther sets up a question then gives us the answer using the Second Article of the Creed:

Now, if you are asked, "What do you believe in the Second Article about Jesus Christ?" answer briefly,

"I believe that Jesus Christ, God's true Son, has become my Lord."

"But what does it mean to become Lord?"

"It is this. He has redeemed me from sin, from the devil, from death, and from all evil. For before I did

9 SA II I 1, 5.

> **not have a Lord or King, but was captive under the devil's power, condemned to death, stuck in sin and blindness" [see Ephesians 2:1–3]. . . .**
>
> **Let this, then, be the sum of this article: the little word *Lord* means simply the same as *redeemer.* It means the One who has brought us from Satan to God, from death to life, from sin to righteousness, and who preserves us in the same. But all the points that follow in this article serve no other purpose than to explain and express this redemption. . . . It explains that He became man [John 1:14], was conceived and born without sin [Hebrews 4:15], from the Holy Spirit and from the virgin Mary [Luke 1:35], so that He might overcome sin. Further, it explains that He suffered, died, and was buried so that He might make satisfaction for me and pay what I owe [1 Corinthians 15:3–4], not with silver or gold, but with His own precious blood [1 Peter 1:18–19]. And He did all this in order to become my Lord.**[10]

Confessing that Jesus is Lord is more than simply saying nice things about Jesus. It means confessing what He has done for us and who He is. The Lutheran Confessions confess Christ wonderfully time and again and help us confess this same Lord.

As we consider different situations in our lives, in our families, in the church, and in the world around us, knowing that God has redeemed us in Christ continues to form us. We are a holy people whose sin has been atoned for. God's wrath against us and our sin has been satisfied by Jesus' blood, which makes peace between God and His people. Through faith, we are a people at peace with God.

10 LC II II 27, 31.

We have a new life in Christ as we are baptized into His death and resurrection and have the name of God Himself placed upon us.

Everything in our lives is about Christ. Every good thing we have comes to us because of Christ and His life lived for us, died for us, and risen for us. The title *Lord* for Jesus is a term of our redemption and what God has done for us in His Son. Luther says a similar thing in his *Lectures on Galatians*. He writes, "For Christ is the Son of God, who gave Himself out of sheer love to redeem me. In these words Paul gives a beautiful description of the priesthood and the work of Christ, which is to placate God, to intercede and pray for sinners, to offer Himself as a sacrifice for their sins, and to redeem them."[11]

Everything comes back to Jesus, who is our Lord. The Lutheran Confessions help form our thinking as we view ourselves as those who belong to Christ. This is the Christian faith that we have been given and what we confess. Since everything about God points us to Jesus, we see how so many other aspects of the Christian faith are connected to Christ. If you have gone through confirmation class, you probably experienced your pastor ask, "Why is it important that Jesus is fully man and fully God?" You likely answered, "He is fully man and God so that He could die and be the perfect sacrifice for my sins and rise again, after dying, on the third day." This echoes the Formula of Concord as it quotes Luther in the article "The Person of Christ" in the Solid Declaration of the Formula of Concord. We see how everything is about Jesus and connected to who He is as the Son of God in examples like this. We also learn how we can confess the importance of the person and work of Jesus, even as young confirmation students.

We get the idea, then, of how understanding Christ is vital to confessing the faith. The Lutheran Confessions teach us this. The Lutheran Confessions not only form us in how we think about confessing Jesus, but they help us see the cohesiveness of the Christian

11 Martin Luther, *Luther's Works*, vol. 26, *Lectures on Galatians, 1535, Chapters 1–4*, ed., trans. Jaroslav Pelikan (St. Louis: Concordia Publishing House, 1963), 177.

faith. All doctrine is a body that is connected. Two good examples of this are found in the Formula of Concord articles "The Holy Supper" and "The Person of Christ."

Article VII and VIII of the Formula of Concord address some controversies that arose surrounding the Lord's Supper and who Jesus is as fully God and fully man. In terms of the Lord's Supper, there were false teachings that included things such as a symbolic understanding and a spiritual eating and drinking of Jesus' body and blood. The writers addressed this topic from the Scriptures and in continuation of the confession made by the church in the Augsburg Confession, the Apology of the Augsburg Confession, the catechisms, and other writings by church fathers and Luther. These articles are beneficial for us as we think about the things of God, but they also help form our thinking about Christ. Pointing out the ramifications of denying that Jesus is truly present in the Lord's Supper should cause us to stop and ask, "What are we saying if Jesus cannot be present in the Lord's Supper?"

Article VII of the Solid Declaration says,

> **Our faith in this article about the true presence of Christ's body and blood in the Holy Supper is based on the truth and omnipotence of the true, almighty God, our Lord and Savior Jesus Christ. This foundation is strong and firm enough to strengthen and establish our faith in all temptations about this article. They overthrow and refute all the Sacramentarians' counterarguments and objections, however agreeable and plausible they may be to our reason. A Christian heart can rest securely and rely firmly on these truths.**[12]

12 FC SD VII 106.

Understanding the Lord's Supper comes back to the words of Christ, who is God in the flesh. In a similar way, Article VIII concerns itself a great deal with the union of the two natures of Christ (divine and human) in the one person. This truth goes throughout the article to show the implications of rightly knowing and confessing who Jesus is as the Son of God. Regarding Jesus in relation to His mother, Mary, the following statement is made:

> **On account of this personal union and communion of the natures, Mary, the most blessed Virgin, did not bear a mere man. But, as the angel <Gabriel> testifies, she bore a man who is truly the Son of the most high God [Luke 1:35]. He showed His divine majesty even in His mother's womb, because He was born of a virgin, without violating her virginity. Therefore, she is truly the mother of God and yet has remained a virgin.**[13]

This explanation of Jesus being born of Mary in the Formula of Concord has been a point of controversy throughout history. Yet this teaching points us back to Jesus, and the Lutheran Confessions affirm the scriptural, historical confession of the church through the centuries and through church fathers and councils such as the Councils of Ephesus (431) and Chalcedon (451). These councils affirmed the scriptural confession that Mary is the "mother of God" (*Theotokos*). We confess this truth about Jesus in the Formula of Concord. We think confessionally and confess Jesus faithfully as we see the implications of what it means that Jesus is fully God and fully man united in one person. His divine nature communicates attributes to the human nature. This means that Jesus can and is truly present in the Lord's Supper, giving us His very real body and

---

13 FC SD VIII 24.

blood, just as His Word says. Likewise, Mary is truly the mother of God, and He who was born of her womb is God in the flesh as Scripture reveals to us in Luke 1.

Our confession of Christ is important. Understanding who God is and what He does brings us great comfort. Let's consider one other instance that shows this truth is at work in a very practical way, this time in terms of understanding Christ and who He is. This time the context involves comforting a mourning husband before his wife's funeral.

There was a faithful, hardworking couple in the community who had been very active in the church. They had their share of health issues over the years, and sadly it got to the point where the wife became ill and died. Of course, her husband mourned. He had lost his wife. Yet even as he mourned, he grieved with hope as 1 Thessalonians 4:13–18 so beautifully puts it.

The day came for the funeral, and he arrived quite early before the rest of his family. He came into the dark sanctuary and sat in the last pew (like a good Lutheran!) praying. As he did, he looked toward the altar, baptismal font, pulpit, and lectern that adorned the front of the sanctuary. My study was off to the side near the front, so it was my practice to walk down a side aisle to get to the narthex before the service to make sure things were in place for people to arrive. This time I walked by the grieving man, and he startled me a bit when I first noticed him. After a brief greeting, he said, "Pastor, I have a question." He said, "I was thinking about my wife dying and all the times we've sat in this place coming to church to hear the Word and take Communion. I know Roman Catholics talk about masses for those who died, and that's wrong, but how do I come here now with her gone?"

His question was a pious one, brought out of grief for his wife and out of love for this place where they sat together receiving the gifts of God. Is receiving the Lord's Supper something we would normally associate with losing a loved one? Maybe or maybe not. Here's the thing, though. For this man sitting in a dark church before his wife's funeral, what he was asking was related to the matter of who Jesus is.

As we mourn the loss of a loved one, the Lord is with us to give us comfort through His Word. As we go to church on Sunday morning, the Lord who called our loved one who died in the faith to Himself is the same Lord who gives us His body and blood in the Lord's Supper. The Lord who physically rose from the dead is the same Lord who promises we, too, shall rise from our graves physically. The Lord who sits at the right hand of the Father is our Brother in the flesh who hears and answers our prayers. Fully God and fully man, Jesus is present with us and for us. He gives His gift of new life to us here on earth, in heaven, and into eternity.

Though this man had lost his wife, God had not changed. Jesus is the same Lord who is fully God and fully man, and who was with him and his wife for so many years as they sat together, heard the Word of God, and then went up to the altar to receive the very body and blood of Jesus. That same Jesus promises He will still be with that grieving man and will continue to deliver those same gifts to him until the Lord calls him to Himself or Jesus returns in glory. Either way, Jesus is the same Lord who understands and shares in our suffering as only He can do. He entered the grave for us and rose victorious from the grave for us.

Sentiment should never define or inform how we view or the reason why we go to the Lord's Supper. There is, however, another comfort in Christ that applies to the situation with the man and his wife. As the Scriptures teach and the Lutheran Confessions confess, Jesus is fully God and fully man. Where He is present in His divinity, He is also present in His humanity. When this widower comes to church and receives the Lord's Supper, He does so in the presence of Jesus. His wife is in the Lord's nearer presence in heaven, but the Lord is the same. There is only one church, and both the widower and his deceased wife are both members; they are just on different sides of the grave. Everything comes back to Jesus—who He is and what He does in life and in death. Because of Jesus, we look forward to the Last Day when all flesh will be raised and when we will forever live with our Lord who will still be fully God and fully man. We will see Him face to face with all the saints in the new creation He will create.

Think about who Jesus is, what He has done, and what He still does. Appreciate how the Lutheran Confessions help form our confession of Him. As we look at the various vocations where God has called us in this life, think about Jesus. Think about how we see and have the great comfort of Jesus in our midst. Knowing that Jesus is risen from the dead and sits at the right hand of the Father, we have the Lord who rules and reigns as our King. He is the same Lord who promises that He is with us always, even to the end of the age. Where Jesus is in His divinity, He is also present in His humanity. Jesus is with us and makes Himself known to us as we have His Word and Sacraments, just as He has promised. The Lord of life who gives life also gives us Himself.

QUESTIONS FOR FURTHER DISCUSSION AND STUDY:

1. Read the affirmative statements of Article VIII, "The Person of Christ," in the Epitome of the Formula of Concord. How is the doctrine of who Jesus is as fully God and fully man connected to other doctrines in the church?

2. Read the affirmative statements of Article III, "The Righteousness of Faith before God." What is the connection between who Jesus is and the righteousness of our faith?

[illegible]RIDERICVS · GVILELMVS IV REX PORTAM [illegible] IN QVA MARTINVS LVTHERVS A DOM MDXVII
[illegible] OCTOBR D XXXI INDVLGENTIIS ROMANIS [illegible] IMPVGNANDIS THESES AFFIXIT LXXXXV
[illegible] FORMATIONIS SACRORVM PRAENVNTIAS [illegible] INCENDIO VASTATAM REFECIT SIGNIS EXORNAVIT
VALVAS EX AERE [illegible] ILLAS THESES [illegible] SCRIBI IVSSIT A DOM MDCCC[illegible]

CHAPTER 3

Is God Involved in My Life?

In a word, enthusiasm dwells in Adam and his children from the beginning to the end of the world. Its venom has been implanted and infused into them by the old serpent. It is the origin, power, and strength of all heresy, especially of that of the papacy and Muhammad. Therefore, we must constantly maintain this point: God does not want to deal with us in any other way than through the spoken Word and the Sacraments. Whatever is praised as from the Spirit—without the Word and Sacraments—is the devil himself.[14]

Confessing who God is connects to other questions: "Is God involved in my life, and if so, does He care about me?" It's not uncommon for people to come to me as their pastor and tell me things like "I wish God would give me some sign. I wish He would tell me He is listening. I wish I knew He was in my life." Knowing who God is and what He has done for us in Christ is a wonderful thing. No one likes the silent treatment. The devil knows this, and he doesn't want us to hear God's Word or have salvation in Christ.

14 SA III VIII 9–11.

Our sinful nature also doubts what God has done and said. We are tempted to think God's Word isn't enough in our lives because we like what we can see in the here and now. We like to trust in things we can understand and feel like we control our lives. Think about how nervous we often get when we must do something outside of our comfort zones. We don't like getting out of our comfort zones because it forces us, in general, to abandon the comfort of familiar experiences and routines. Getting out of our comfort zones may force us to learn to do something that is completely foreign and unusual to us. In order to operate outside of what is comfortable to us, we have to look outside of ourselves.

God's Word, what we read and hear, often sounds so foreign to us and the world around us. Not only that, but when we encounter it, God exposes things. Through the Word, God shows us what we really have come to fear, love, and trust in, and God calls those out to us and directs us away from those things. The Solid Declaration of the Formula of Concord confesses, "Because unbelief is the root and wellspring of <all sins that must be rebuked and reproved>, the Law rebukes unbelief also."[15] We sinners don't like this, but this is what God says to us. He speaks to us in terms of who we are as sinners. God is very much concerned about our lives here and now and speaks to us here and now, but we, in our sinful nature, want to close our eyes and ears to Him as He speaks to us through His Word. The Bible teaches us that God works through means, the Word and Sacraments, to give us Christ and His benefits. The Lutheran Confessions help form us to see our confidence in Christ through these means of grace.

Article IV of the Augsburg Confession unpacks the doctrine of justification. In many ways, this is the doctrine of the Christian faith, all the other topics are articles of that faith. The church stands or falls on the doctrine of justification. Succinctly yet profoundly, Article IV states this:

15 FC SD V 17.

Our churches teach that people cannot be justified before God by their own strength, merits, or works. People are freely justified for Christ's sake, through faith, when they believe that they are received into favor and that their sins are forgiven for Christ's sake. By His death, Christ made satisfaction for our sins. God counts this faith for righteousness in His sight (Romans 3 and 4 [3:21–26; 4:5]).[16]

Our righteousness before God is the righteousness of Christ, whom God has imputed or counted to us through faith. In this way, our faith in Christ is our righteousness before God. That righteousness frees our consciences. We see that we cannot save ourselves. But God, in Christ, has redeemed us by His perfect obedient life and His sacrificial death to atone for our sin, which rightly is under God's wrath and condemnation.

We have peace with God through faith in Christ (see Romans 5:1–2). The devil, the world, and our own fallen flesh, however, try to take our eyes off Christ. God, though, is rich in His mercy toward us and has delivered His promises to us in tangible ways. He is at work in our lives, and we cling to these means of grace as the instruments by which we cling to Christ.

Article V of the Augsburg Confession continues the thread of Article IV on justification:

So that we may obtain this faith, the ministry of teaching the Gospel and administering the Sacraments was instituted. Through the Word and Sacraments, as through instruments, the Holy Spirit is given [John 20:22]. He works faith, when and where it pleases God [John 3:8], in those who hear

16 AC IV 1–3.

the good news that God justifies those who believe that they are received into grace for Christ's sake. This happens not through our own merits, but for Christ's sake.

Our churches condemn the Anabaptists and others who think that through their own preparations and works the Holy Spirit comes to them without the external Word.[17]

Salvation has been accomplished and won for us in Christ. God first cares about us, redeeming us in Christ. Flowing from this, He still takes care of us, continually delivering the forgiveness of sins, life, and salvation to us by the means of grace. Questions that arise in our lives concerning if God is still working are answered as the Scriptures are read and preached in our midst and as we receive the Sacraments. God is faithful, giving us His gifts in everything we may encounter. It is the same Jesus who "is the same yesterday and today and forever" (Hebrews 13:8).

It is important for us to think about these means of grace and how they form us. The way God delivers His gifts to us not only puts things into perspective or sets our priorities, but it forms how we live. Everything in our faith is derived from the reception of God's gifts in the Word and Sacraments. God is at work and attaches His promises in these gifts.

Even though we may doubt God's work and involvement in our lives, God still bestows on us His gifts that deliver peace to our consciences. Consider this statement from the Apology of the Augsburg Confession:

It is well known that we have made clear and praised the benefit of Absolution and the Power of the Keys.

17 AC V 1–4.

Many troubled consciences have derived comfort from our teaching. They have been comforted after they heard that it is God's command, no, rather the very voice of the Gospel, that we should believe the Absolution and regard it as certain that the forgiveness of sins is freely granted to us for Christ's sake. We should believe that through this faith we are truly reconciled to God. This belief has encouraged many godly minds and, in the beginning, brought Luther the highest praise from all good people.[18]

This quote is from the article on confession. Notice the language of troubled consciences and comfort. Our sinful minds and hearts trouble our consciences for any number of reasons. These include doubt, the sin that accuses us, and temptation that assaults and is working to lead into despair and other great shame and vice (to borrow language from the Small Catechism). Conscience can be a deafening voice that drives us to despair when we face these things. God, though, in His great mercy, speaks His Word of comfort to us in Holy Absolution. He gives peace to our consciences by forgiving our sins for the sake of Christ and delivering this to us through the means of words of forgiveness.

Pastors can attest to the very pointed application of the Gospel in individual or private confession and absolution. When someone comes to the pastor, he or she comes as one approaching Christ for peace and comfort as only Christ can give. The person confessing his or her sins speaks a general confession followed by an optional confession of specific, troubling sins. After this confession, the pastor stands and places his hand on the person, speaks the person's name, and says, "In the stead and by the command of my Lord Jesus Christ I forgive you all your sins in the name of the Father and of the

18 Ap XI 59.

✠ Son and of the Holy Spirit. Amen."[19] Besides actually delivering the forgiveness of sins, these words leave no doubt in this person's mind that Christ has died for this person, forgiven his or her sins, and makes this person to stand righteous before the throne of God. Does God care about the lives of Christians? Is He involved in those lives? Confession and absolution, along with Baptism, the Lord's Supper, and the Holy Scriptures, give a resounding, "Absolutely!" The means of grace, be they read, preached, or taught, silence this doubt and grant troubled consciences great peace and comfort.

The means of grace also form how we confess the faith to others close to us and in the world around us. Knowing how God works through the means of grace gives us great comfort, forming how we speak about Jesus and where He is found for our benefit. We live each day as Christians, knowing that God is for us in Christ, and He is most assuredly at work in our lives. We also invite and point others to where God has promised to be found in these saving means.

God also forms how we see Him working in our lives on a daily basis when we pray and mediate on the Lord's Prayer. Think about how many things are included in the introduction, seven petitions, and conclusion of the Lord's Prayer as described in both the Small and Large Catechisms. In particular, the Large Catechism helps us think about who we are and what God does for us each day in the promises God makes in the Lord's Prayer. It reminds us of what we actually confess as we pray to our Lord. As we walk through a few sections of this part of the Lutheran Confessions, we will see how God forms us to think confessionally about His work in our daily lives.

Luther begins the discussion of the Lord's Prayer with a general theology of prayer. In a brief definition, Luther writes, "To call upon God's name is nothing other than to pray [c.g., 1 Kings 18:24]."[20] This stems from the understanding that God commands us to pray

---

19 *LSB*, p. 293.

20 LC III 5.

and promises to hear us. Command and promise, then, summarize the theology of prayer taught by the Scriptures. We not only have the command to pray, but we also have that wonderful promise that God will hear and answer our prayers.

Prayer is directed to God and connected to the right use of the name of God as we understand in the Second Commandment. The language of Father and children in relationship to prayer is used throughout the Lutheran Confessions. We are His children who ask for and receive from our gracious Father something so basic as our daily bread. Prayer is a serious matter and is formed by God's Word, and we are to pray with confidence, knowing that God is listening. As we in humility consider who we are and who our God is in the Lord's Prayer, God shapes us to reverently trust that He listens and answers our petitions.

The sermonic nature of the Large Catechism speaks to us as hearers of the Word of God. When we pray the Lord's Prayer, we know that God cares for us. For example, Luther writes,

Indeed, the human heart is by nature so hopeless that it always flees from God and imagines that He does not wish or desire our prayer, because we are sinners and have earned nothing but wrath [Romans 4:15]. Against such thoughts (I say), we should remember this commandment and turn to God, so that we may not stir up His anger more by such disobedience. For by this commandment God lets us plainly understand that He will not cast us away from Him or chase us away [Romans 11:1]. This is true even though we are sinners. But instead He draws us to Himself [John 6:44], so that we might humble ourselves before Him [1 Peter 5:6], bewail this misery

and plight of ours, and pray for grace and help [Psalm 69:13].[21]

It is a humbling thing, then, to pray these petitions. As we do, we look outside of ourselves and see that our only help is found in the One who hears and answers us as only He can. God cares so much for us. We can't ever realize or thank God enough for just how merciful and gracious He is in giving us what we need.

In his explanation of the Fourth Petition, "Give us this day our daily bread," Luther again preaches to us from God's Word, showing and admonishing us to realize and thank God for all His daily care. He says,

You see, in this way, God wishes to show us how He cares for us in all our need and faithfully provides also for our earthly support. He abundantly grants and preserves these things, even for the wicked and rogues [Matthew 5:45]. Yet, He wishes that we pray for these goods in order that we may recognize that we receive them from His hand and may feel His fatherly goodness toward us in them [Psalm 104:28; 145:16]. For when He withdraws His hand, nothing can prosper or be maintained in the end.[22]

Even the wicked are cared for by God in this earthly life. This care doesn't save them, to be sure, but it is still a testament to the fact that God cares for His creation. He cares for us by giving us daily bread. He provides for us through His creation. He uses fathers and mothers to work and bring food to their families. He uses farmers to tend the land and bring in the harvest the Lord provides. He

21 LC III 10–11.

22 LC III 82–83.

uses neighbors to help others in times of trial and scarcity to help take care of one another. He uses governments to protect citizens and punish evil so that we may live peaceful and quiet lives in faith toward God and in love toward our neighbors. This is all contained in this short petition of the Lord's Prayer.

Luther begins the discussion of the Fifth Petition, "And forgive us our trespasses as we forgive those who trespass against us," by saying, "This part now applies to our poor miserable life. Although we have and believe God's Word, do and submit to His will, and are supported by His gifts and blessings, our life is still not sinless. We still stumble daily and transgress because we live in the world among people"[23] Luther's point hits home. We know all too well that we sin against our neighbors and our neighbors sin against us. This stresses the reality that we need to pray to God and call upon Him for mercy. Asking God to not hold our sin against us means praying in faith and trusting in the person and work of Christ as our mediator. Praying the Fifth Petition confesses our confidence on where we stand before the Father on account of the Son.

In the Sixth Petition, "And lead us not into temptation," we pray for protection against our fallen flesh, the world, and the devil, which daily seek to take us away from God. As Christians, we have deliverance from these things in Christ. He perfectly obeyed the Law of God and overcame the assaults of the devil. However, we face temptation differently. We fight against it and resist it. We are armed against these evil temptations by God's promises, and we pray that we would not fall away from the faith but have the victory. We run and take hold of God's Word and pray the Lord's Prayer for deliverance amid the temptations in this life. Likewise, the Seventh Petition, "But deliver us from evil," is related to the Sixth as it prays for deliverance from the devil. Praying this petition, we confess God's desire for us to run to Him daily and seek His help. We have our deliverance and victory in Him alone.

---

23 LC III 86.

That little word *Amen* at the end of the Lord's Prayer contains so much. We pray in confidence because our faith trusts the promises that God will hear and answer our petitions on account of Christ. We do not doubt but know with certainty that the Lord doesn't close His ears to our cries. Instead, our dear Father listens and gives out of His grace. Like all prayer to God, the Lord's Prayer is rooted in the wonderful promises of the Gospel. We do not despise these promises of forgiveness, life, and salvation but gladly send our prayers before God as sweet incense rising to His throne.

God most definitely is involved in our lives and cares for us in ways that we can't even begin to count. Baptized into Christ, we get up each morning as those who belong to Him and as His dear children. We run to God's promises and gather where He has promised to be for us in our daily lives. God gives us forgiveness, life, and salvation in His Word and Sacraments. God gives us daily bread and the faith to see, through the Scriptures, how He is still working in our lives and even using us to work in the lives of others. It is truly a joy to behold all of this, think about it, and confess that God is involved in our lives and cares for us.

QUESTIONS FOR FURTHER STUDY AND DISCUSSION:

1. How do the Small and Large Catechisms' examinations of the three articles of the Apostles' Creed form and shape our understanding and confession of God working in our lives?
2. Articles V and VI of the Epitome and Solid Declaration of the Formula of Concord are about the Law and Gospel and the third use of the Law, respectively. Look at those articles and what they confess about God's Word. In what ways do Law and Gospel inform and play a part in how we see God at work in our lives?

SECTION II

Who Am I?

I am who I say I am . . . or at least that's what I've been told.

There are a lot of voices crying out trying to tell us who we are and what defines us. Our own minds and hearts seek to answer "Who am I?" The doctrine of creation, however, shows us exactly who we are. We discover this in relationship to God, who created us and invites us to call Him "our Father." God's Word also reveals that we have sinned against Him and that the devil, the world, and our own fallen flesh want nothing more than to tear us away from Christ.

Yet, on account of Christ, we are forgiven. Baptized into Him, we are a new creation, and we have life that sees and knows ourselves as His own. We confess that we are His people, living in faith toward God and in love toward our neighbors, who need us just as we need them.

CHAPTER 4

Who Is Man?

And God saw everything that He had made, and behold, it was very good. (GENESIS 1:31)

We believe, teach, and confess that there is a distinction between man's nature and original sin. This applied not only when he was originally created by God pure and holy and without sin [GENESIS 1:31]*, but it also applies to the way we have that nature now after the fall. In other words, we distinguish between the nature itself (which even after the fall is and remains God's creature) and original sin. This distinction is as great as the distinction between God's work and the devil's work.*[24]

Who is man, and why can't I decide what this means? When we look at ourselves, we are tempted to think we can define who we are in this life. This inward-focused model seems to be a given in the world around us. The Scriptures, though, teach us that we do not determine who we are as humans. The Lutheran Confessions, confessing the Scriptures, help form our thinking about what it means to be a creature of God, both in this world and in the life to come. We read in the book of Genesis that God created everything, and at the moment of creation, it was all good because it had been

24 FC Ep I 1.

created by Him. That's the thing about what God creates: it is good. It is very good, just as God is good. To be God's creatures is to see our very existences as good because we are God's good handiwork.

The First Article of the Apostles' Creed confesses who we are as creatures of God. It does so by focusing on our relationship with our Creator. Our Creator is not some idea or abstract notion of a deity. He the one true God we call Father. That's nothing insignificant. When we consider who we are in this world, that relationship is in fact extremely significant. God is our Father who has created us and still takes care of us, giving and providing all we need in both body and soul. "He does all this out of pure, fatherly, divine goodness and mercy, without any merit or worthiness in me."[25]

There are a lot of voices and opinions in the world today that try to tempt us to disbelieve God's Word concerning who we are as His creatures. Even something so basic to our existences as being a man or a woman is under attack. We are bombarded with images and messages that try to distort or just downright deny the truth of God's Word, which teaches about the great joy and freedom found in being who God has created us to be as male or female.

To be a man or a woman, at its very core, is about the mercy and care of God. The fact that God made us either a man or a woman is good thing; it is part of His very good design. He is the one who has done this and made us, as Scripture says, "So God created man in His own image, in the image of God He created him; male and female He created them" (Genesis 1:27). Our essence as a man or a woman goes back to God, our Father, who made us. When we try to locate our identity outside of who God has created us to be, we're not only sinning, but we are also robbing ourselves of true consolation, comfort, and confidence in who we are. Our beings as a man or a woman rest in God, who alone is good and knows us personally. As we consider this, we see how the Lutheran Confessions are a treasure for us in this fallen world. They rightly confess God's design

25 SC II First Article.

for who man is and who he is not. They help us not only rejoice in who we are in this life but also how to confess the Holy Scriptures to our neighbors in our daily lives.

A good starting point in the Lutheran Confession as we think about being who God has created us to be is the First Article of the Apostles' Creed. It confesses, "I believe in God the Father Almighty, maker of heaven and earth." In that short statement, we are included in this confession. In the Large Catechism, Luther beautifully preaches, "We emphasize the words 'Creator of heaven and earth.' But what is the force of this, or what do you mean by these words, 'I believe in God the Father Almighty, maker of heaven and earth?' Answer: 'This is what I mean and believe, that I am God's creature [2 Corinthians 5:17]. I mean that He has given and constantly preserves [Psalm 36:6] for me my body, soul, and life, my members great and small, all my senses, reason, and understanding, and so on.'"[26] Understanding that we are creatures of God is tremendously important.

To unpack this so we can best understand and confess faithfully what God has revealed, we need to start making some distinctions about humanity. One of the issues facing the writers of the Formula of Concord concerned the nature of humanity and what this means in relation to our original sin. For the writers, the doctrine of man originates with God creating and forming him. God created man, and woman from man, on the sixth day of creation, and mankind is the pinnacle of God's creation. The only thing made in God's image in all of God's creation is man. That's quite something. To be a man or a woman is precious in the sight of God and sets us above everything else in all creation. Creation is so vast that we can't even begin to comprehend its scope, and the reality that God counts humanity as the pinnacle of that creation is humbling.

When God formed Adam from the dust, He formed him in His image. Adam was the only being in all of God's vast and magnificent

26 LC II 12–13.

creation who could say that about himself. Likewise, Eve (whose name means "life") was created from the side (or rib) of Adam. God's care was at work for Adam and Eve as He created them for each other. God created Adam first and Eve from Adam second, laying out an order for men and women to live together in this world. God delights when men and women live together in marriage harmony within His created order. God made humans as men and women and has great pleasure in His creation. This relationship is very personal. We are known by God, and we are His creation.

The Lutheran Confessions know and rightly confess this reality about our humanity. They also address when things got ugly: when sin entered the picture at the fall of man. The devil sought to pervert God's creation and all that was good. It is important that God's truth forms our thinking so that we can distinguish between God creating man good and sin corrupting that good creation. Because we are all corrupted by sin from conception, we can't rightly think about our humanity on our own. We need God's Word to reveal His truth to us and form us.

We rightly confess that we are "by nature sinful and unclean" in the Divine Service (e.g., *LSB*, p. 151). We have this original or hereditary sin passed down to us from Adam. Romans 5:12, 18–19 teaches us, "Therefore, just as sin came into the world through one man, and death through sin, and so death spread to all men because all sinned. . . . Therefore, as one trespass led to condemnation for all men, so one act of righteousness leads to justification and life for all men. For as by the one man's disobedience the many were made sinners, so by the one man's obedience the many will be made righteous."

Since the fall into sin, man's nature is corrupt. No one conceived and born after Adam and Eve fell into sin is without sin. No one. The only exception (which is not really an exception like we use the term, as His is both true God and true man) is Jesus. He was conceived by Holy Spirit in the womb of the virgin Mary. He is fully God and fully man yet alone without sin. This leads us to an important point in this whole discussion about creation and humanity. Jesus is man but without sin. Just because He is human does not mean that He is a sinner. Also, Jesus came to do God's work and to separate sin from man. The Lutheran Confessions confess that Jesus is also fully God, so He can do work God alone can do. Jesus is both man without sin and God, who is able to do God's work, and this is good.

Let's go back to that fact that God created man, Adam, yet God did not create or bring about sin. God's creation is good, and sin is what has corrupted man and brought about all its consequences. Sin leads ultimately to death, which is the righteous punishment against sin. The Epitome of the Formula of Concord rightly confesses, "God created the body and soul of Adam and Eve before the fall. But He also created our bodies and souls after the fall. Even though they are corrupt, God still acknowledges them as His work, as it is written in Job 10:8, 'Your hands fashioned and made me.' (See also Deuteronomy 32:18; Isaiah 45:9–10; 54:5; 64:8; Acts 17:28; Psalm 100:3; 139:14; Ecclesiastes 12:1.)"[27]

The devil knows all too well how good God's creation is and God's delight in making and preserving humanity. Even though our first ancestors fell, God delights in the fact that He has created us and we are His. It's not surprising, then, when the devil goes after these truths and tries to redefine or obscure how people talk about God's human creatures. Satan does so to mock the Creator and make God's creatures think they are more important than they are and that they can create or redefine themselves.

Pride is a deadly thing. It's eternally deadly. Throughout history, pride has been seen as the chief vice or deadly sin. So many of humanity's sinful thoughts, words, and deeds have pride at their core. Proverbs 16:18 bluntly states, "Pride goes before destruction, and a haughty spirit before a fall." Pride is a form of idolatry.

The epistle of Jude tells us something about the fallen angels as this relates to pride and God's order of creation. They were not

27 FC Ep I 4.

content with what God created them to be; they wanted a different order to God's creation. God writes through Jude:

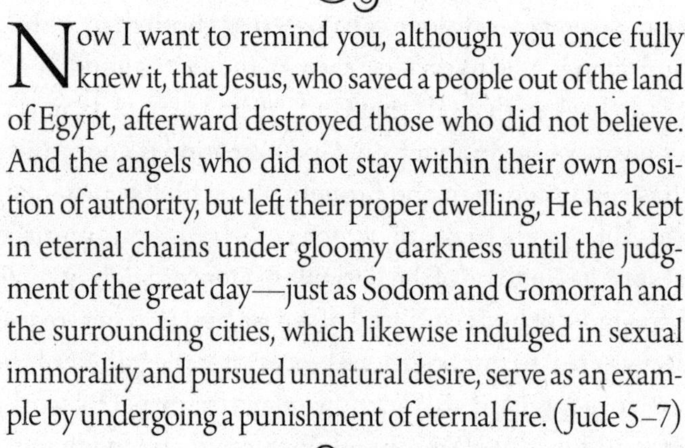

Now I want to remind you, although you once fully knew it, that Jesus, who saved a people out of the land of Egypt, afterward destroyed those who did not believe. And the angels who did not stay within their own position of authority, but left their proper dwelling, He has kept in eternal chains under gloomy darkness until the judgment of the great day—just as Sodom and Gomorrah and the surrounding cities, which likewise indulged in sexual immorality and pursued unnatural desire, serve as an example by undergoing a punishment of eternal fire. (Jude 5–7)

The Bible is full of instances and examples of God's people, and all creation, taking pride in themselves. They look to themselves and their own sinful desires to define themselves and justify what they do. As the passage from Jude shows us, the angels are no exception. Angels are creatures, and the ones who fell with Satan were not content with who God made them to be. Like us humans, they desired a different order of creation, which was not in line with God's.

God shows another instance of what happens when creatures think they have the power to create in Romans 1:18–27:

For the wrath of God is revealed from heaven against all ungodliness and unrighteousness of men, who by their unrighteousness suppress the truth. For what can be known about God is plain to them, because God has shown it to them. For His invisible attributes, namely, His eternal power and divine nature, have been clearly perceived, ever since the creation of the world, in the things that have been made. So they are without excuse. For although they knew God, they did not honor Him as

> God or give thanks to Him, but they became futile in their thinking, and their foolish hearts were darkened. Claiming to be wise, they became fools, and exchanged the glory of the immortal God for images resembling mortal man and birds and animals and creeping things.
>
> Therefore God gave them up in the lusts of their hearts to impurity, to the dishonoring of their bodies among themselves, because they exchanged the truth about God for a lie and worshiped and served the creature rather than the Creator, who is blessed forever! Amen.
>
> For this reason God gave them up to dishonorable passions. For their women exchanged natural relations for those that are contrary to nature; and the men likewise gave up natural relations with women and were consumed with passion for one another, men committing shameless acts with men and receiving in themselves the due penalty for their error.

There are a lot of things going on in this section of Scripture, but it's important for us to read, mark, and inwardly digest what God says to us. First, we see how God reveals things about Himself in creation so that no one is left with an excuse. This means that no one can rightly claim there is no God. God's creation reveals certain things about God, like His power. Theologians call this a natural knowledge of God. There are also things in the natural order of creation pertaining to right and wrong that are written on the hearts of men. This is part of what is called natural law. The natural knowledge of God and natural law, however, are not the saving knowledge of God and do not reveal the Gospel to us. No one is saved apart from Christ. No one knows who God is and what He has done in Christ through natural knowledge. The true, full nature of God is only revealed to us by the Holy Spirit through the Holy Scriptures. This is called God's special revelation.

Second, this passage from Romans reveals that being a creature of God is different from being the Creator. Being a man created by God means that we are not God. There is someone outside of ourselves—God—who brought us into being and gave us life. This reality humbles God's human creatures. Jesus says, "For everyone who exalts himself will be humbled, and he who humbles himself will be exalted" (Luke 14:11). Humility is the opposite of pride. For the Christian, humility is the way of life that confesses and turns us from sin and drives us to cling to Christ alone for our redemption. In humility, we hear the Word of God and hold fast to it, knowing that it is a "lamp to [our] feet and a light to [our] path" (Psalm 119:105).

Moving past the Romans passage, we see that the devil is a murderer, a liar, and "the father of lies" (John 8:44). So just as he knows that God has created us and what God creates is good, he tries to get us to attribute sin to God. He wants us to think that if we have desires toward sinful behavior or desires to be different from who God has created us to be (as a man or a woman), then these desires must be from God. After all, God created us, right? These desires must be from God, right? The thing about the devil, though, is that he is not very creative. The devil is always up to his old tricks of trying to get humans to doubt God and His Word. He tries to call evil good and good evil, and he gets us to do the same. God warns us of this in Isaiah 5:20–21: "Woe to those who call evil good and good evil, who put darkness for light and light for darkness, who put bitter for sweet and sweet for bitter! Woe to those who are wise in their own eyes, and shrewd in their own sight!" Sinful desires that deny God's order of man and woman are not from God. They come from a sinful corruption of God's good order for His human creatures, not from God Himself. Jesus came to die on the cross and rise again to forgive our sins and, as He has promised, to return to raise the dead and restore God's creation to an incorruptible state. That is the Christian hope.

The Scriptures and the Lutheran Confessions help us see who we are as God creatures: that He is our Creator and has redeemed us in Christ. All questions about who we are find their answer in the Lord who has created us, redeemed us, and sanctifies us. We look outside of ourselves to God to see who we are, which is a wonderful thing. When the world, the devil, and our fallen flesh try to get us to doubt who we are as God's people, God silences them and speaks the truth in His Word, bringing us comfort. He tells us who we are and to trust who He is. He has created us to be in this world, and denying His truth about His human creatures harms His creatures not just spiritually but also physically, even unto everlasting death.

As God's people, we also find joy in God's created order. We delight in being men and women and participating in God's creation according to how God has created us to live in His order. One place the Lutheran Confessions drive this point home, though in a bit of an indirect way, is in the article "The Marriage of Priests" in the Apology of the Augsburg Confession.

At the time of the writing of the Lutheran Confessions, forbidding priests to marry was a more recent innovation in the church. It also went against the clear words of Scripture. While it was obvious during the writing of the Augsburg Confession that this issue was in reference to marriage and the office of the ministry, other implications also can be made. We see how forbidding priests to marry rejects the order of God's creation of men and women and His institution of marriage. Melanchthon wrote,

Second, because this creation, or divine ordinance, in humanity is a natural right, jurists have said wisely and correctly that the union of male and female belongs to natural right. Natural right is unchangeable. Therefore, the right to contract marriage must always remain. Where nature does not change, that ordinance which God gave nature does not change.

It cannot be removed by human laws. Therefore, it is ridiculous for the adversaries to babble that marriage was commanded in the beginning, but is not now. This is the same as if they would say, "Formerly, when people were born, they were born with gender; now they are not. Formerly, when they were born, they brought with them natural right; now they do not." No craftsman (*Faber*) could produce anything more crafty than these foolish things. They were created to dodge a natural right.[28]

Denying priests the right to marriage denies not only marriage itself but who God created us to be as men. This corresponds to pastors today. God's creation is just that: it's His creation, and it is good. Marriage, likewise, is a good and great estate that was established by God before sin entered the world. It is also good for a man and a woman to desire each other. Not in lust, but in marriage. God's design is that a man should desire a woman as his wife and a woman should desire a man as her husband. They should not just view the opposite sex as sexual objects.

It is also good and a right when there is order in this marriage according to God's institution. A man is to be the head of the woman, and the woman is to submit to her husband. In Ephesians 5, God shows us this order and the beautiful picture we have in this estate and what it reflects:

Wives, submit to your own husbands, as to the Lord. For the husband is the head of the wife even as Christ is the head of the church, His body, and is Himself its Savior. Now as the church submits to Christ, so also wives should submit in everything to their husbands.

28 Ap XXIII 9–10.

> Husbands, love your wives, as Christ loved the church and gave Himself up for her, that He might sanctify her, having cleansed her by the washing of water with the word, so that He might present the church to Himself in splendor, without spot or wrinkle or any such thing, that she might be holy and without blemish. In the same way husbands should love their wives as their own bodies. He who loves his wife loves himself. (Ephesians 5:22–29)

This order of creation for men and women in marriage is also seen in other aspects of creation. Another example (among many) comes from 1 Timothy 2:12–15: "I do not permit a woman to teach or to exercise authority over a man; rather, she is to remain quiet. For Adam was formed first, then Eve; and Adam was not deceived, but the woman was deceived and became a transgressor. Yet she will be saved through childbearing—if they continue in faith and love and holiness, with self-control." God's order of creation for men and women exists in the church in places like the office of the ministry, where only men are permitted to occupy the office of pastors.

The order of creation for men and women does not diminish the value or love God has for men or women in creation. It teaches us and forms us to live our lives according to God's will. As Christians, then, we delight in this order and see and join in saying with God that it is "good" not only in the whole of creation but in our lives personally.

We rejoice in what God establishes. How absurd it is to deny what God created and has established. In the Apology of the Augsburg Confession, Melanchthon rightly and prophetically wrote that denying the truth of God's creation is as absurd as someone or something trying to say people are not born a certain sex, that is, born either a man or a woman. Luther wrote a similar thing in the Smalcald Articles regarding the marriage of priests: "Now, neither we nor they have been given the power to make a woman out of a man or a man out of a woman, or to nullify either sex. So they have had no authority to separate such creatures of God, or to forbid them from living honestly in marriage with one another."[29]

As Christians, we know who God has created us to be and confess this in our lives. We uphold the institutions He has established, like marriage, which are part of His creation. We rejoice in God's creation and order and celebrate who we are in relation to Him. God cares for us as our Father. The Large Catechism preaches to us,

> **Further, we also confess that God the Father has not only given us all that we have and see before our eyes, but He daily preserves and defends us against all evil and misfortune [Psalm 5:11]. He directs all sorts of danger and disaster away from us. We confess that He does all this out of pure love and goodness, without our merit, as a kind Father. He cares for us so that no evil falls upon us.**[30]

Think about that as you consider who you are in this world. There is no person in the world who is living now, or will be living, whom God has not created. God does good for all and has reconciled the world to Himself in Christ (2 Corinthians 5:19). For those who believe in Him, God gives the right and privilege to call Him Father and to know that He will take care of them as their dear Father.

Our consolation and confidence are found in Christ. Jesus took on human flesh. That's significant for us even now. The Epitome of the Formula of Concord summarizes this well and forms our thinking when it confesses,

29 SA III XI 2.

30 LC II 17.

Furthermore, God's Son has received this human nature [John 1:14], but without sin. Therefore, He did not receive a foreign nature, but our own flesh in the unity of His person. In this way He has become our true Brother. Hebrews 2:14 says, "Since therefore the children share in flesh and blood, He Himself likewise partook of the same things." Again, "For surely it is not angels that He helps, but He helps the offspring of Abraham. Therefore He had to be made like His brothers in every respect, . . . yet without sin" [2:16; 4:15]. In the same way, Christ redeemed human nature as His work, sanctifies it, raises it from the dead, and gloriously adorns it as His work. But original sin He has not created, received, redeemed, or sanctified. He will not raise it, adorn it, or save it in the elect. In the <blessed> resurrection original sin will be entirely destroyed [1 Corinthians 15:51–57].[31]

Who is man? God answers this question and reveals to us who we are in His creation. Thanks be to God for who He has created us to be and the confidence He gives us as we trust His Word. It is good, in fact, very good, to be who God made us and to uphold and live within the order God has established. Rather than trying to look inward for our identity, we look to God, who has created us to be men and women. In this, we see the care of God in our daily lives as well as the redemption we have in Jesus.

31 FC Ep I 5–6.

QUESTIONS FOR FURTHER DISCUSSION AND STUDY:

1. Seeing the distinctions made in Article I in the Solid Declaration of the Formula of Concord, how can we understand statements like "God created us to live"? How does this inform how we view death? Is it a "natural" part of life?

2. How can things like the quotes from the articles on the marriage of priests help form how we confess God's Word faithfully and speak to hot-button issues today regarding marriage or even being a man or a woman?

CHAPTER 5

What's the Deal with Sin?

Our churches teach that since the fall of Adam [Romans 5:12], all who are naturally born are born with sin [Psalm 51:5], that is, without the fear of God, without trust in God, and with the inclination to sin, called concupiscence. Concupiscence is a disease and original vice that is truly sin. It damns and brings eternal death on those who are not born anew through Baptism and the Holy Spirit [John 3:5].

Our churches condemn the Pelagians and others who deny that original depravity is sin, thus obscuring the glory of Christ's merit and benefits. Pelagians argue that a person can be justified before God by his own strength and reason.[32]

What's the deal with sin? If being a creature of God is so great, then why would anyone disobey God? What even is sin, really, and how does this affect who we are as people? The answers to these questions involves returning to the fundamental issue of living in a fallen world. Sin is serious, deadly serious. Part of what the Lutheran Confessions do is help us ask the right questions and realize who we are in this sinful world.

32 AC II 1–3.

We must first define what sin is and what it is not. This is especially helpful to consider, because the more we look at what sin is, the more we see how much it affects our lives, our neighbors, the world around us, and so many other things. The Smalcald Articles contain a section on sin, connected to the First Commandment, that gets to the very core of the issue. Luther confesses:

Here we must confess, as Paul says in Romans 5:12, that sin originated from one man, Adam. By his disobedience, all people were made sinners and became subject to death and the devil. This is called original or the chief sin.

The fruit of this sin are the evil deeds that are forbidden in the Ten Commandments [Galatians 5:19–21]. These include unbelief, false faith, idolatry, being without the fear of God, pride, despair, utter blindness, and, in short, not knowing or regarding God. Also lying, abusing God's name, not praying, not calling on God, not regarding God's Word, being disobedient to parents, murdering, being unchaste, stealing, deceiving, and such.

This hereditary sin is such a deep corruption of nature that no reason can understand it. Rather, it must be believed from the revelation of Scripture.[33]

It's helpful to see how Luther lays out and forms our thinking in this part of the Lutheran Confessions. He helps us see what it means that we are sinful and how this sin is manifested in our lives. Sin is a hereditary condition that has been passed down to us from our earthly father and mother, who themselves are sinners.

33 SA III I 1–3.

Romans 3:10–12, citing Psalm 14 and Psalm 53, teaches us, "None is righteous, no, not one; no one understands; no one seeks for God. All have turned aside; together they have become worthless; no one does good, not even one."

There's a saying pastors will often teach their confirmands: "We are not sinners because of sin. We sin because we are sinners." This lines up with what the Holy Scriptures teach us and what Luther says in the Smalcald Articles.

One intertwined concept with original sin is *concupiscence*. This will be defined later, but it is important to look at the historical context in which the Lutheran Confessions were written first. Concupiscence has been a point of controversy from the time of the writing of the Lutheran Confessions up to this day. In the Apology of the Augsburg Confession, Melanchthon addresses a response to the Augsburg Confession by the Roman Catholic Church called the Confutation. The theologians of the papal church denied that concupiscence is sin. Concupiscence, for them, was more of a weakness or a defect in human nature brought about by the fall. On the surface, this might not sound like a big deal or might seem to be a matter of splitting hairs. In fact, concupiscence addresses a vital aspect of our sinful condition and dare not be rejected.

This denial of concupiscence as sin was not in accord with what the church had taught for centuries. The denial of concupiscence in the Confutation even went against many of the Roman Catholics Church's trusted writers. Above all, though, this denial goes against what God teaches us about sin in the Scriptures. Understanding concupiscence helps us see the all-encompassing scope of sin, which is more than just a deficiency. Instead, sin is a big deal and permeates all throughout our lives. So what is this concupiscence the Lutheran Confessions teach, and how do they help us understand it?

By way of a short definition, Melanchthon wrote in the Apology, "Concupiscence is not only a corruption of physical qualities, but also, in the higher powers, a vicious turning to fleshly things."[34] Sin corrupts us even to the extent that our thoughts and desires are turned toward sin and against righteous law. Concupiscence is this inborn turning of our natures to sin. Jesus teaches this in the Sermon on the Mount. In Matthew 5, Jesus says, "You have heard that it was said to those of old, 'You shall not murder; and whoever murders will be liable to judgment.' But I say to you that everyone who is angry with his brother will be liable to judgment; whoever insults his brother will be liable to the council; and whoever says, 'You fool!' will be liable to the hell of fire. . . . You have heard that it was said, 'You shall not commit adultery.' But I say to you that everyone who looks at a woman with lustful intent has already committed adultery with her in his heart" (Matthew 5:21–22, 27–28).

God inspired Paul to reveal this to us as well. Three passages from Scripture in particular that stand out are 1 Corinthians 2:14; Romans 7:13–25; and 1 John 2:16. In 1 Corinthians 2:14, Paul writes, "The natural person does not accept the things of the Spirit of God, for they are folly to him, and he is not able to understand them because they are spiritually discerned." Romans 7 is rich with so many things that teach us about, on the one hand, the nature and scope of our sin, and, on the other, the mercy and deliverance we have only in Christ. For instance, Paul writes,

Did that which is good, then, bring death to me? By no means! It was sin, producing death in me through what is good, in order that sin might be shown to be sin, and through the commandment might become sinful beyond measure. For we know that the law is spiritual, but I am of the flesh, sold under sin. For I do not understand my own actions. For I do not do what I want, but I do the very thing I hate. Now if I do what I do not want, I agree with the law, that it is good. So now it is no longer I who

34 Ap II 25.

> do it, but sin that dwells within me. For I know that nothing good dwells in me, that is, in my flesh. For I have the desire to do what is right, but not the ability to carry it out. For I do not do the good I want, but the evil I do not want is what I keep on doing. Now if I do what I do not want, it is no longer I who do it, but sin that dwells within me.
>
> So I find it to be a law that when I want to do right, evil lies close at hand. For I delight in the law of God, in my inner being, but I see in my members another law waging war against the law of my mind and making me captive to the law of sin that dwells in my members. Wretched man that I am! Who will deliver me from this body of death? Thanks be to God through Jesus Christ our Lord! So then, I myself serve the law of God with my mind, but with my flesh I serve the law of sin. (Romans 7:13–25)

Finally in 1 John 2:16, God says, "For all that is in the world—the desires of the flesh and the desires of the eyes and pride of life—is not from the Father but is from the world."

What these passages show us, and what the Lutheran Confessions confess, is that sin is so serious and so encompassing that even the things we desire and know to be sinful still have sway in our lives. We continually fall into sin because of the old sinful nature we still possess. Even if we don't act on something sinful, the very thought and desire to sin is itself sinful, as Jesus teaches in Matthew 5.

Scripture and the Lutheran Confessions form our thinking about sin. It is tempting for us to attribute the source of the desires we have to God, our Creator, in an attempt to somehow make Him the reason for our sin. The Bible, however, clearly teaches us this is not the case. God is not the source of our sinful desires. In fact, the exact opposite is true. God shows us who we are, exposing our sinful hearts, when He holds up His Law before our faces. God defines sin; we do not. Our consciences are held captive to God's Word and not the other way around. Just because we desire something does not make it good. Jesus says in Matthew 15:18–20, "But what comes out of the mouth proceeds from the heart, and this defiles a person. For out of the heart come evil thoughts, murder, adultery, sexual immorality, theft, false witness, slander. These are what defile a person. But to eat with unwashed hands does not defile anyone."

When we take these passages to heart and examine ourselves, we see the broad scope of sin in our lives and in the world around us. Sin is real and manifests itself in real, concrete ways. Everyone has a concept of sin in some way, shape, or form. This is why it is important for us to listen to what God says and think about how God's Word forms us. Why? Because our sinful nature is ready, willing, and capable to try and downplay sin or take control of the driver's seat in our lives, defining the terms and conditions for what is right and wrong.

One way our old human nature likes to operate is to either seek to redefine sin or take the edge off of sin so that it seems to be less deadly. This tactic is a form of self-justification or trying to make ourselves righteous before God apart from Christ. God clearly shows us, though, that this is a lie, and to say otherwise is to make Him a liar. John writes,

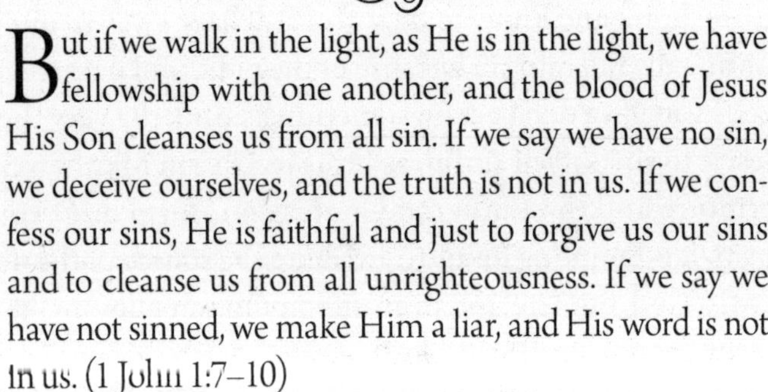

> But if we walk in the light, as He is in the light, we have fellowship with one another, and the blood of Jesus His Son cleanses us from all sin. If we say we have no sin, we deceive ourselves, and the truth is not in us. If we confess our sins, He is faithful and just to forgive us our sins and to cleanse us from all unrighteousness. If we say we have not sinned, we make Him a liar, and His word is not in us. (1 John 1:7–10)

The world around us attempts to deflect, redefine, or simply write sin off. Knowing the seriousness of sin in our own lives, we are to be on our guard against these temptations. Attempts from the devil and the world to get us to normalize sin abound and are serious for us and our children. God warns us and calls us to be faithful. God calls us to speak His Word of truth about sin in the vocations He has given us. God's judgment about what is good and what is sinful is revealed to us in His Law. He shows us what is rightly due for sin: death. Sin is a big deal; God knows this and takes it seriously.

We dare not fear to call out sin for what it is and to do so confidently. It is God who has revealed this to us, and He commands us to speak the truth about sin and judgment. We do so in love for our neighbors and for the sake of their restoration before God and eternal salvation. We also do this in humility. Galatians 6:1–3 teaches us, "Brothers, if anyone is caught in any transgression, you who are spiritual should restore him in a spirit of gentleness. Keep watch on yourself, lest you too be tempted. Bear one another's burdens, and so fulfill the law of Christ. For if anyone thinks he is something, when he is nothing, he deceives himself." We take sin seriously because we love our neighbor. God doesn't want people to perish eternally. Ezekiel 33:11 tells us, "As I live, declares the Lord God, I have no pleasure in the death of the wicked, but that the wicked turn from his way and live."

When we must speak words that point out sin and call people to repentance, we do it according to our roles and responsibilities in life. When we do, we must faithfully speak back what God has said to us. Parents rebuke, forgive, and teach their children because they don't want them to live in their sin. They want them to cling to Jesus and His forgiveness and live the new life God has given and called them to in the waters of Holy Baptism. When we must speak, we don't render judgment from our own sinful hearts but speak and confess God's judgment as He has revealed in the Scriptures. A parent who disciplines his child does so in love. Failure to do so is a failure to love. 1 Corinthians 13:6 tells us that love "does not rejoice at wrongdoing, but rejoices with the truth."

Think about how God has created us. Since humanity's fall into sin, we have inherited sin; the actual sins we do or good things we fail to do are fruits of this sin. Also think about how sin has ruined everything in our lives. The devil, the world, and our fallen flesh want nothing more than for us to think lightly about sin or underestimate its scope in our lives. In light of this, where is our comfort? Paul answers, "Wretched man that I am! Who will deliver me from this body of death? Thanks be to God through Jesus Christ our Lord!" (Romans 7:24–25).

Confessing Christ, we see the real problem with sin and what this means as we live in this world. As we take sin seriously and understand the havoc it wreaks in the world, God leads us by His Word to find comfort and peace solely in Christ. The Apology sums this up well when it states, "The knowledge of original sin is absolutely necessary. The magnitude of Christ's grace cannot be understood unless our diseases are recognized. <Christ says in Matthew 9:12 and Mark 2:17, 'Those who are well have no need of a physician.'> The entire notion that a person is righteous is mere hypocrisy before God. We must acknowledge that our heart is, by nature, destitute of fear, love, and confidence in God."[35]

Time and again, the Lutheran Confessions beautifully preach the redemption we have in Christ. In many ways, an overarching theme of the Book of Concord is our consolation in Christ. It is consolation for the sinner who has been redeemed by His blood. It is consolation for the sinner to see where his righteousness is found, in his Lord, and how this is received through faith through the means of grace, the Word and Sacraments. God consoles us, which is nothing short of miraculous. Consider this passage from the Solid Declaration:

We unanimously believe, teach, and confess the following about the righteousness of faith before God, in accordance with the comprehensive summary of

35 Ap II 33.

our faith and confession presented above. A poor sinful person is justified before God, that is, absolved and declared free and exempt from all his sins and from the sentence of well-deserved condemnation, and is adopted into sonship and inheritance of eternal life, without any merit or worth of his own. This happens without any preceding, present, or subsequent works, out of pure grace, because of the sole merit, complete obedience, bitter suffering, death, and resurrection of our Lord Christ alone. His obedience is credited to us for righteousness.

These treasures are brought to us by the Holy Spirit in the promise of the Holy Gospel. Faith alone is the only means through which we lay hold on, accept, apply, and take them for ourselves. This faith is God's gift [Ephesians 2:8–9], by which we truly learn to know Christ, our Redeemer, in the Word of the Gospel and trust in Him. We trust that for the sake of His obedience alone we have the forgiveness of sins by grace, are regarded as godly and righteous by God the Father, and are eternally saved.[36]

This quote preaches the Gospel. God knows that sin is a big deal. He knows that it must be answered for, as is His right, and He has done so in Christ. The obedience of Jesus consoles us over and above our disobedience and sinful condition. A few lines later, the authors continue:

Therefore, the righteousness that is credited to faith or to the believer out of pure grace is Christ's obedience, suffering, and resurrection, since He has made

36 FC SD III 9–11.

> **satisfaction for us to the Law and paid for <expiated> our sins. Christ is not man alone, but God and man in one undivided person. Therefore, He was hardly subject to the Law (because He is the Lord of the Law), just as He didn't have to suffer and die for His own sake. For this reason, then, His obedience (not only in His suffering and dying, but also because He was voluntarily made under the Law in our place and fulfilled the Law by this obedience) is credited to us for righteousness. So, because of this complete obedience, which He rendered to His heavenly Father for us by doing and suffering and in living and dying, God forgives our sins. He regards us as godly and righteous, and He eternally saves us. This righteousness is brought to us by the Holy Spirit through the Gospel and in the Sacraments. It is applied, taken, and received through faith. Therefore, believers have reconciliation with God, forgiveness of sins, God's grace, sonship, and are heirs of eternal life.**[37]

The Lutheran Confessions show us a very freeing way of understanding what is truly at stake when it comes to sin—and eternal life. They also reveal what it means to have someone who has atoned for our sins, Jesus Christ, who frees us from their eternal consequences. As Christians, by grace through faith, we are righteous in the sight of God. The mercy of God in Christ is astounding. His obedience to the Father and the Law is perfect. He is without sin. He is righteous. His obedience to God's Law, both active as He fulfilled the Law and passive as He suffered and died for our sake, is complete. The righteousness of Christ is counted to us through faith.

For us Christians, sin no longer defines who we are. Rather, we see sin as something that has been defeated. We are no longer slaves

37 FC SD III 14–16.

to sin but are forgiven and righteous. We have a new life as baptized children of God, daily drowning our old sinful man and delighting in what God teaches us is to be the new life of His children. We are free to live as Christians and rejoice in what our Lord has done and continues to do. Think about all of this. What a joy it is to have a new life in Christ, who has redeemed us from sin, death, and the devil.

QUESTIONS FOR FURTHER STUDY AND DISCUSSION:

1. How does understanding the connection between concupiscence and sin help us understand what we see around us in the world and its views of sin? How does this help us to be on guard and see things for what they are in accordance with God's Word?
2. Read the Large Catechism on the significance of Baptism, Part IV, paragraphs 64–86. In what ways does the Large Catechism help form our understanding of our attitude toward sin as Christians in opposition to our new life in Christ?
3. Read the Solid Declaration of the Formula of Concord, Article I, paragraphs 1–15. Which distinctions help form our understanding of what sin is and is not? How can these be used as we confess this article in our lives?

CHAPTER 6

What about Our Neighbors?

In God's sight faith is what really makes a person holy and serves Him alone [Romans 4:3–5], but the works are for the service of people.[38]

What does it mean to live together with the people around us? The Scriptures teach us that our neighbors need us and we need them. We don't live in isolation. God saw that it was not good for Adam to be alone, so God made a helper fit for him (see Genesis 2:18). Likewise, God has created and put us together in this world. As we discussed in chapter 4, when God created humans and established humans to live in community, He did so in an orderly way. Foundationally, this order concerning all our neighborly relationships goes back to Adam and Eve in the Garden of Eden. That is why it has been said that our closest neighbor is our spouse. If God wills it, He will give children within that union of husband and wife. The family, and the order within it between husband, wife, parents, children, and, by extension, the whole web of connected extended family relationships, is the basic structure of life in society and the world.

38 LC I 147.

How we serve as Christians in the world in love toward our neighbor, then, is an important topic. This was one of the issues at the time of the Reformation; it formed the backdrop of some of the articles within the Lutheran Confessions. Topics like monasticism and the medieval doctrine of the office of the ministry redefined a godly Christian life. These topics confused God's order for service to neighbor, turning it into a new order whereby the ordinary life of a Christian was subpar to that of a monk, priest, or nun. Within this monastic system, it was falsely taught that one had to abandon one's family and God-given vocations to live a righteous life.

The Smalcald Articles, among other writings, mention how even something good like monasteries, which started out providing education and services to others, had by the time of Luther turned into something detrimental. Luther wrote, "If these institutions will not serve this purpose, it is better to abandon them or tear them down than have their blasphemous, humanly invented services regarded as something better than the ordinary Christian life and the offices and callings ordained by God."[39]

God's order in creation is good. In it, God uses people to provide for one another. To borrow a phrase from Luther's Post-Communion Collect in *Lutheran Service Book*, within this order, our lives are lived in "faith toward [God] and in fervent love toward one another." As we think about our lives in this world, then, we consider not only where we fit into this order but how we live in relationship to one another.

Luther confesses the Scriptures in the Large Catechism, and we can and do use these documents to help us think through our various roles in life. Luther writes on the Fourth Commandment in the Large Catechism:

We must, therefore, impress this truth upon the young [Deuteronomy 6:7] that they should think of their parents as standing in God's place. They

39 SA II III 2.

> **should remember that however lowly, poor, frail, and strange their parents may be, nevertheless, they are the father and the mother given to them by God. Parents are not to be deprived of their honor because of their conduct or their failings. Therefore, we are not to consider who they are or how they may be, but the will of God, who has created and ordained parenthood. In other respects, people are, indeed, all equal in God's eyes. But among humans there must necessarily be this inequality and ordered difference. Therefore, God commands this order to be kept, that you obey me as your father [Matthew 5:48], and that I have the supremacy.**[40]

This teaching extends even further and across all walks of life in what Lutheran theologians call the "three estates." God gives different offices, stations, and positions of authority to different people, and this is a godly thing. One often overlooked section of the Small Catechism, the Table of Duties, is helpful in forming our understanding of how God has placed us in our lives in relation to each other. In the Table of Duties, Luther walks through various passages in the New Testament, primarily the Epistles, showing how God has established these various estates and stations in life within them. These also teach us what we owe to one another living in these estates. For example, within the church, we need a pastor to preach to us and administer the Sacraments. Hearers, also within the church, are to listen and obey their preachers. The pastors are to be faithful and held to what God teaches the life of one should be.

Think about all the different ages and stages humans go through. Whether young or old, married, single, or widowed, in all these things, we are God's children. No matter the station, God teaches us who we are in this life. The end of the Table of Duties summarizes

40 LC I 108.

this well and forms our whole thought process as we look at God's commandments and His will, which instructs our new life in Him.

For Young Persons in General

Likewise, you who are younger, be subject to the elders. Clothe yourselves, all of you, with humility toward one another, for "God opposes the proud but gives grace to the humble." Humble yourselves, therefore, under the mighty hand of God so that at the proper time he may exalt you. (1 Peter 5:5–6)

For Widows

She who is truly a widow, left all alone, has set her hope on God and continues in supplications and prayers night and day, but she who is self-indulgent is dead even while she lives. (1 Timothy 5:5–6)

For All in Common

The commandments . . . are summed up in this word: "You shall love your neighbor as yourself." (Romans 13:9) "First of all, then, I urge that supplications, prayers, intercessions, and thanksgivings be made for all people." (1 Timothy 2:1)

Let each his lesson learn with care, and all the household well shall fare.[41]

As we consider ourselves and our neighbors, then, we really see how practical the Lutheran Confessions are for our lives. We saw in chapter 4 how articles that seem very specific, like "The Marriage of Priests" in the Augsburg Confession (AC XXIII), its Apology

41 SC Table of Duties.

(Ap XXIII XI), and the Smalcald Articles (SA III XI), extol the estate of marriage and confess the very practical reasons why marriage should be upheld as a truly good and holy thing instituted by God.

Thinking confessionally about our neighbors and ourselves—and our eternal relationship to God—is an important task. We are sinners, but thanks be to God, who has redeemed us by Christ. His resurrection from the dead proclaims God's victory over sin and death for us, and we are now justified, or declared righteous, before God. God's Law accuses us in our sin, but as Christians, baptized children of God, it also teaches God's will for our lives. The Formula of Concord rightly calls this the "third use of God's Law" (FC SD VI).[42] "The Law is a mirror in which God's will and what pleases Him are exactly portrayed. This mirror should be constantly held up to the believers and be diligently encouraged for them without ceasing."[43]

The Ten Commandments teach us Christians of God's good will for our lives, and we delight in what God teaches us. The first table of the Law, Commandments One through Three, addresses our relationship and life toward God. Commandments Four through Ten address God's will for the relationship between us and our neighbors. We call this the second table of the Law. Now, ultimately, even the second table of the Law is related and part of our relationship with God. However, the second table addresses the things we readily see before us relating to our neighbors.

In many ways, the Large Catechism is a sort of handbook for Christians, showing us the God-pleasing way of living in relationship to our neighbors. Walking through these Commandments is a helpful exercise we can keep coming back to as we continually examine our lives and seek to conform our new lives in Christ to what our Lord teaches us. The Large Catechism's explanations of these Commandments are formed by the Word of God and help us think confessionally about our neighbor in the world. As we

---

42 The heading of this article in the Formula of Concord could also be translated as the "three uses of the law." Regardless, God's Law reveals His will for our lives as Christians.

43 FC SD VI 4.

look in overview at the Commandments, their practicality shines through. We can almost hear Luther preaching to us, even now in the twenty-first century.

The Fourth Commandment, which is discussed in a long section of the Large Catechism, begins the discussion of the second table of the Law. God teaches us how we are to relate to our neighbor. This, too, is an orderly thing. God has established fathers and mothers as a special office within His creation. "To the position of fatherhood and motherhood God has given special distinction above all positions that are beneath it: He does not simply command us to love our parents, but to honor them."[44]

The family is of utmost importance. Luther says all other authority "flows and is born from the authority of parents."[45] God has established this order that fathers have authority over their children and household. What is due to fathers is not just love but honor. Likewise, fathers are commanded to raise up their children according to the will of God. This is a high calling. It is no wonder that the fallen powers of the devil, the world, and our sinful flesh continually attack fatherhood and this order of the family in society so much. Destroying the headship of a father over the household brings about the opposite of order: chaos.

Valuing the office of parents brings special blessings, as this commandment contains a promise. Christian parents and children are instructed by God to follow what the Lord commands in this commandment so life will go well with them. Good things happen when parents are both honored and raise their children up in the fear, love, and trust of God. It is no coincidence that each section of the Small Catechism begins, "As the Head of the Family Should Teach Them in a Simple Way to His Household."[46]

---

44 LC I 105.

45 LC I 141.

46 SC I.

Luther also extends the Fourth Commandment to include other ways we are to show honor in the world. Honor is also given to civil authorities as God's instruments to govern society. Spiritual fathers (pastors) are due a "double honor,"[47] Luther states, as they have charge over souls. In all these things, the Lord's order is for our good. We are called to honor our father and mother as parents are called to raise their children to be Christian people.

The Fifth Commandment continues to draw us outside of ourselves. We are to consider our neighbor and his well-being. God protects people in this and the other commandments. Luther says, "God well knows that the world is evil [Galatians 4:1], and that this life has much unhappiness. Therefore, He has set up this and the other commandments between the good people and the evil."[48] Our call as Christians is not to harm our neighbor but to protect and defend him no matter how young in the womb or near death he may be in this life. This is another example of Luther teaching how God both prohibits something in the commandment and instructs us in our new life. This is further explained at the end of the section on the Fifth Commandment (LC I 196–198). Here, Luther points us to God's Word on what true good works and a new holy life in Christ look like. As we read this section, we see how God's Commandments inform us on where we are to look to for instruction for the Christian life.

In the explanation of Sixth Commandment, we notice the thought progression of Luther as it relates to this commandment on human sexuality. The neighbor is addressed personally. Luther states, "Then they proceed to talk about the person nearest him, or the closest possession next after his body, namely, his wife. She is one flesh and blood with him [Genesis 2:23–24], so that we cannot inflict a higher injury upon him in any good that is his."[49] Toward the close of this explanation, Luther addresses the inner nature of what God

47 SC, Table of Duties

48 LC I 183.

49 LC I 200.

commands. The totality of God's Law and the understanding of the whole person is significant as we consider how we are living in love toward our neighbor. Luther notes how chastity is more than an outward act. It is also a matter of the human heart. Luther shows the practical purpose of guiding young people in this commandment so that they desire the married estate, know it is a blessed estate, and see that marriage pleases God (see LC I 217–18). Luther also demonstrates how a Christian husband or wife, as opposed to an unbelieving husband or wife, has a new relationship to this Law. Within this vocation, or rather this estate, Luther locates the place of good works for the Christian: "Here you have again precious, indeed, many and great good works. You can joyfully boast about them, against all churchly estates chosen without God's Word and commandment."[50]

The Seventh Commandment concerns itself with temporal property. It is far-reaching in scope. Like the Fifth Commandment, there is a command to do no harm to the neighbor but instead to help the neighbor in his property and possessions. The attitude of the Christian is one of service, not self-promotion. Toward the close of this section on the Seventh Commandment, there is another statement that helps us think about and form how we live in love toward our neighbors. Luther reiterates,

> **This is enough of an explanation of what stealing is. Let the commandment not be understood too narrowly. But let it apply to everything that has to do with our neighbors. . . .**
>
> **Whoever now seeks and desires good works will find here more than enough to do that are heartily**

50 LC I 221.

acceptable and pleasing to God. In addition, they are favored and crowned with excellent blessings.[51]

God's Law is good, and we do well to follow what it teaches, not in an attempt to save ourselves but because, for Christians, good works are fruits of our faith. In Christ, we desire what our Lord commands and believe what He teaches is good.

Commandments Eight through Ten continue in this line of showing concrete ways our faith is lived out in love toward our neighbors. We see these real things we are to do to for real people in our lives. Our neighbors need us, and we need them. Serving the needs of our neighbors is good and right in this world.

Living in all three estates (church, family, and secular), Christians occupy themselves with the Ten Commandments and what they teach about daily life. Luther states, "Just occupy yourself with them. Try your best. Apply all power and ability. You will find so much to do that you will neither seek nor value any other work or holiness."[52] The new man doesn't create new works to be done for God. Instead, God has already placed these works before the new man in the Commandments so that they may flow from his faith in God his Father.

Luther ends this section on the Ten Commandments by teaching how "the First Commandment is to shine and gives its splendor to all others."[53] Each commandment, in both tables, comes back to the First. We are to understand that the Commandments are all connected to who God is and what God desires for His people. Christians do well to teach the Commandments to their children and exercise them daily.

God's handiwork and order is a wonderful thing. The Lutheran Confessions confess God's order and help form how we see ourselves,

---

51 LC I 250, 252.

52 LC I 318.

53 LC I 326.

according to God's Word, in relation to our neighbors. God cares for His people, and we serve as His instruments to take care of our neighbors. This begins with our spouse, if we are married, and our children, and then spirals outward. God delights when we live in love toward our neighbors as He calls us to do and teaches us what this looks like in the vocations. The Lutheran Confessions, especially the Large Catechism's unpacking of the Ten Commandments, form us to both think confessionally and live out this confession before God and the world.

QUESTIONS FOR FURTHER DISCUSSION AND STUDY:

1. Read the Apology, Article V, paragraph 68. Why does Melanchthon state that we are to do good works? How does this help us think about the role of good works in our lives?
2. Read the Epitome, Article IV, paragraphs 5–15. How does who we are as new people in Christ relate to the relationship we have to our neighbors and God's Law?

SECTION III

What Is the World to Me?

After confessing who we are and who God is, what do we say about the world around us? How do the Lutheran Confessions help us see the world rightly? What does it mean to live in the world as the baptized people of God looking forward to the life to come? Blessedly, as Christians living in this world, we are provided the answers by God's Word. We know what the world needs, or rather we know who the world needs. It needs Jesus just as we do. This is our confession as the church in this world. We live out our days clinging to the means of grace with eyes toward our sure and certain future with our Lord and His saints forever.

CHAPTER 7

What Does Baptism Mean for My Life in This World?

Think about it. Imagine there was a doctor somewhere who understood the art of saving people from death or, even though they died, could restore them quickly to life so that they would afterward live forever. Oh, how the world would pour in money like snow and rain. No one could find access to him because of the throng of the rich! But here in Baptism there is freely brought to everyone's door such a treasure and medicine that it utterly destroys death and preserves all people alive.

We must think this way about Baptism and make it profitable for ourselves. So when our sins and conscience oppress us, we strengthen ourselves and take comfort and say, "Nevertheless, I am baptized. And if I am baptized, it is promised to me that I shall be saved and have eternal life, both in soul and body."[54]

54 LC IV 43–44.

What does it mean to be a baptized child of God in this world? That's an important question we continually need to ask ourselves. The world is dying, and so are we; we know the seriousness of sin and its consequences. Each day, or even each breath, could be our last one on this earth. It's not a pleasant thing to think about, is it? We don't want to think about our own mortality, or we at least try to avoid thinking about it at all costs. Then a pandemic hits, or a loved one dies suddenly, and we are forced to see death and all its ugliness on the screen or right before our eyes.

The fallen world is corrupted by sin and its consequences. These consequences have a way of redefining our lives that can lead us to despair or to falsely believe there is no meaning in anything. We get up in the morning, do our thing during the day, go to bed in the evening, and then when the alarm goes off the next morning, it's repeat and repeat until the day comes when we don't get up anymore. That thought by itself can be terrifying. It should be for those outside of salvation in Christ.

For Christians, though, things are different. We think differently. We talk differently. We even live our daily lives differently no matter how humdrum they may seem. This is all different because we are baptized, and that means everything. To be baptized is to see God has a claim and stake on us and our lives. He's invested in us, and we have His name permanently on our heads. He's in this baptized relationship with us for the long haul, and He tells us how this is all going to end when we face our last day. This relationship defines our daily lives as His children.

Baptism is such an important thing for our life in Christ. Really, it is the foundation for who we are as Christians. We will often hear the phrase "Remember your Baptism." That is a great statement to hear; we should remember our Baptisms. The danger exists, though, when we only view our Baptisms as a past event rather than an event that (though it did happen in the past) still has ramifications today and into eternity. Understanding this can be difficult because we easily lose sight of our current state of being baptized.

The devil, the world, and our sinful nature try to take our focus off of our Baptisms into Christ and weigh us down with the cares and pleasures of this world.

Unpacking what God has given us in our Baptisms, and the significance of this in our daily lives, is a lifelong endeavor. In the Large Catechism, Luther writes, "Therefore, every Christian has enough in Baptism to learn and to do all his life. For he has always enough to do by believing firmly what Baptism promises and brings: victory over death and the devil [Romans 6:3–6], forgiveness of sin [Acts 2:38], God's grace [Titus 3:5–6], the entire Christ, and the Holy Spirit with His gifts [1 Corinthians 6:11]. In short, Baptism is so far beyond us that if timid nature could realize this, it might well doubt whether it could be true."[55] When we start to think about all that Baptism is and gives us, it sounds almost too good to be true, but this makes it more wonderful.

The Lutheran Confessions help us see how our lives are impacted in very concrete ways by our Baptisms in the name of God. They help us think confessionally about what God has done in our Baptisms and how this is significant in our lives. They help form us as we walk in faith toward God and in love toward one another through this world. These are documents of the church, and the church lives in this world with real people and real-life situations. The original authors of the Lutheran Confessions lived in the real world, too, centuries ago. They saw the state of the church, God's people, ignorance, false teaching, suffering consciences, and so much else, and from God's Word, they sought to confess Christ and the Christian faith faithfully to the people of their day.

The Lutheran Confessions highlight the importance of Baptism, and all the means of grace, in the life of God's people. For a time leading up to the Reformation, Baptism had taken a back seat for Christians. It was more a preparatory or initial part of the Christian life. It was one plank that people had in their salvation progress.

55 LC IV 41–42.

Luther and the other reformers saw these errors as well as the great comfort that had been robbed from God's people when Baptism was viewed this way. Looking back to the Scriptures, the writers of the Lutheran Confessions put Baptism back into Christians' lives. To them, Baptism is something to unpack and live out through this life into the next.

A great example of this mindset, which teaches about the lives of Christians as the baptized people of God, is found in the Preface to the Large Catechism. Luther writes about the situation not just among the Christian people but among the pastors who have been given charge to teach and encourage them in their baptized life. He writes,

For example, the Holy Spirit is present in such reading, repetition, and meditation. He bestows ever new and more light and devoutness. In this way the catechism is daily loved and appreciated better, as Christ promises in Matthew 18:20, "For where two or three are gathered in My name, there am I among them."

Besides, catechism study is a most effective help against the devil, the world, the flesh, and all evil thoughts. It helps to be occupied with God's Word, to speak it, and meditate on it, just as the first Psalm declares people blessed who meditate on God's Law day and night (Psalm 1:2). Certainly you will not release a stronger incense or other repellant against the devil than to be engaged by God's commandments and words, and speak, sing, or think them [Colossians 3:16]. For this is indeed the true "holy water" and "holy sign" from which the devil runs and by which he may be driven away [James 4:7].

> **Now, for this reason alone you ought gladly to read, speak, think, and use these things, even if you had no other profit and fruit from them than driving away the devil and evil thoughts by doing so. For he cannot hear or endure God's Word. God's Word is not like some other silly babbling, like the story about Dietrich of Berne, for example. But as St. Paul says in Romans 1:16, it is "the power of God." Yes indeed, it is the power of God that gives the devil burning pain and strengthens, comforts, and helps us beyond measure.**[56]

So how does this help us? The Lutheran Confessions always address Baptism with the goal of giving us certainty in what Christ has accomplished by His life, death, and resurrection. There are fine theological points and nuances to be made, to be sure, and those have their place in the Lutheran Confessions, but we can read, hear, teach, and preach them and be certain that they focus on what God has done for us in Holy Baptism.

In some ways, then, the Lutheran Confessions are a handbook on what it means to be baptized into Christ. This book containing documents from the sixteenth century (and prior in the case of the Creeds) is a significant, true treasure. As we approach reading the Lutheran Confessions, we always have Christ's benefits to us through Baptism in mind. As we are taught the Lutheran Confessions by others or read it in our own time, God forms us by His Word. Think about that! Here are these documents from so many years ago, yet they are still speaking to and teaching us. The subject of Baptism in the Book of Concord is directly about our Baptisms. This is about us and about all of God's people, the church.

---

56 LC Longer Preface 9–11.

So what about it in terms of who we are as the baptized people of God? Let's go back to the quote from the Large Catechism at the beginning of this chapter, which brings up the image of a doctor who can raise the dead. Luther invites us to think about what it would look like. In today's world, can we imagine all the social media posts and news stories this doctor would draw and the level of a celebrity he would be? A doctor who raises the dead! What an unthinkably wonderful thing. People would pay thousands or even millions of dollars just to have one visit with this doctor.

That's Baptism! That is what we have in our Baptisms because of Christ, who is the Great Physician of body and soul. We don't have to imagine what our Baptisms are and give. We have this reality now. We are receiving and living out the blessings of the Great Physician all day every day. As Luther says, though, "think about it" (e.g., LC IV 43). Think about what it means to be baptized and to have forgiveness and healing. That means even if we face death, we have life. God has called us out of the darkness of sin, death, and the kingdom and power of the devil into the light and His kingdom, which knows no end. God places His name upon us. When we have God's name, we have everything that goes along with this name above all names. Though we don't necessarily know what our immediate future holds, because of our Baptisms, we know what the end will be and what our future eternity will entail.

Luther's explanation of Baptism in the Large Catechism is profound. Our "doctor" is Jesus, who raises the dead, even as He Himself is risen. When we face times of illness, suffering, and death, we face them as those who have a doctor who says to us in our Baptisms, "Don't worry. I have healed you, and you will not die but live forever." Thinking about Baptism this way means thinking about our lives now as people who will live forever. This is a game changer and forms a new way of thinking, speaking, and living.

The Lutheran Confessions show us how Baptism connects us to Christ. Jesus lived in perfect obedience to the Law of God and suffered the death we deserved. He died for our sins and was raised for our justification. The Holy Spirit has worked our God-given faith for us and receives and lays hold of all that Christ has done for us. As baptized children, then, the righteousness of Jesus is now our righteousness through faith in Him. Once again, look at the Solid Declaration of the Formula of Concord, Article III. This article nicely summarizes what it means to be baptized into Christ:

> **Therefore, the righteousness that is credited to faith or to the believer out of pure grace is Christ's obedience, suffering, and resurrection, since He has made satisfaction for us to the Law and paid for <expiated> our sins. Christ is not man alone, but God and man in one undivided person. Therefore, He was hardly subject to the Law (because He is the Lord of the Law), just as He didn't have to suffer and die for His own sake. For this reason, then, His obedience (not only in His suffering and dying, but also because He was voluntarily made under the Law in our place and fulfilled the Law by this obedience) is credited to us for righteousness. So, because of this complete obedience, which He rendered to His heavenly Father for us by doing and suffering and in living and dying, God forgives our sins. He regards us as godly and righteous, and He eternally saves us. This righteousness is brought to us by the Holy Spirit through the Gospel and in the Sacraments. It is applied, taken, and received through faith. Therefore, believers have reconciliation with God, forgiveness of sins, God's grace, sonship, and are heirs of eternal life.**[57]

57 FC SD III 14–16.

Think about the work of Christ and think about Baptism. Baptism delivers Christ's righteousness to us and recreates us so that we are free to truly live and enjoy life in this world as only a Christian can do. "[God] regards us as godly and righteous, and He eternally saves us." That's the confidence our Baptisms give us and the outlook we have in life. We see the world differently because of our Baptisms. Both the scenario of the doctor in the Large Catechism and the excerpt from the Formula of Concord show us God's perspective on how He sees His baptized children on account of Christ. The Lutheran Confessions serve as a lens through which we see the world and our lives, with eyes that have been created anew and transformed by our Baptisms.

The formation plays out daily as we think about the healing and life we have in those baptismal waters. The Solid Declaration of the Formula of Concord makes this point about our baptismal lives, which further shapes our perspective and thinking: "After God (through the Holy Spirit in Baptism) has kindled and caused a beginning of the true knowledge of God and faith, we should pray to Him without ceasing [1 Thessalonians 5:17]. We should ask that through the same Spirit and His grace, by means of the daily exercise of reading and doing God's Word, He would preserve in us faith and His heavenly gifts, strengthen us from day to day, and keep us to the end. For unless God Himself is our schoolmaster, we can study and learn nothing that is acceptable to Him and helpful to ourselves and others."[58]

Making daily use of our Baptisms, or making it "profitable for ourselves," as Luther writes in the Large Catechism (IV 44), describes our lives in Christ. Toward the end of this section of the Large Catechism, Luther writes, "For this reason let everyone value his Baptism as a daily dress [Galatians 3:27] in which he is to walk constantly. Then he may ever be found in the faith and its fruit, so that he may suppress the old man and grow up in the new. For

58 FC SD II 16.

if we would be Christians, we must do the work by which we are Christians."[59] That's another interesting image: Baptism is our "daily dress." A Christian never has to worry about what he is going to wear every morning, in this sense at least. He is dressed in his Baptism!

Baptism grants both life and a life lived out confidently in sure and certain hope. As we've seen in the Lutheran Confessions quotes in this chapter, this formation happens daily in very real ways. This, too, goes back to how God's Word fundamentally defines our days. Paul wrote by divine inspiration to the Colossians, "Let the word of Christ dwell in you richly, teaching and admonishing one another in all wisdom, singing psalms and hymns and spiritual songs, with thankfulness in your hearts to God. And whatever you do, in word or deed, do everything in the name of the Lord Jesus, giving thanks to God the Father through Him" (Colossians 3:16–17).

Our state of being washed clean in the saving waters of Baptism is inseparable from both God's Word and our being students of His Word or, to use the biblical term, disciples. The baptismal life is a life of hearing God's Word and knowing it works in our lives as God sends it out to accomplish His purposes (see Isaiah 55:10–11).

God's Word exhorts us to "pray without ceasing" (1 Thessalonians 5:17). This is nothing other than calling upon the name that God has placed upon us in Baptism. Baptized into the name of God, we can rightly with all boldness and confidence call upon God, our Father. Each day, we arise as new creatures in Christ who live in this world, except unlike unbelievers, we live as sons and daughters of God who have the ear of God Himself in prayer. Our days are ordered by His governance and care. Whatever our tasks may be or whatever we may face in life, the name of the Holy Trinity is on our foreheads and the Creator and Sustainer of all things is our Father, who treats us as His dear children. Our lives are free, and as the baptized people of God, they have order and purpose.

59 LC IV 84–85.

The Lutheran Confessions, especially the Small and Large Catechisms, help us see and appreciate what God has given us in our Baptisms. We can read and use the Lutheran Confessions to help us faithfully confess what our baptismal lives mean in accord with God's Word. Our lives are an unpacking and a living out of what God has so graciously given to us in those blessed baptismal waters. For people who bear the holy name of God through Baptism, the Lutheran Confessions help form a lifelong study of our Christian identities. The Table of Duties at the end of the Small Catechism is a great example of this as we think about the vocations God has called us to live in this world in the church, in our families, and in society. God teaches us what the Christian life looks like and guides us along our paths so that we will glorify Him in what we say and do, honor His name, and love our neighbor as Christ first loved us.

For further reading: Small Catechism, Part IV, Baptismal Book, Table of Duties; Large Catechism, Part IV; Epitome of the Formula of Concord, Article IV, paragraphs 5–10

QUESTIONS FOR FURTHER DISCUSSION AND STUDY:

1. In what ways is the phrase "Remember your Baptism" a helpful confession of who God has called us to be?
2. How can the Lutheran Confessions be considered a handbook for the baptized?
3. What other connections can be made between Baptism and various other articles of faith as we see them lived out in our lives?

RIDERICVS · GVILELMVS · IV · REX · PORTAM · IN QVA MARTINVS LVTHERVS · A · DOM · MDXVII
M · OCTOBR · D · XXXI · INDVLGENTIIS · ROMANIS · IMPVGNANDIS · THESES · AFFIXIT · [illegible]
REFORMATIONIS · SACRORVM · PRAENVNTIAS · [illegible] INCENDIO · VASTATAM · REFECIT · SIGNIS · EXORNAVIT
[illegible] INSCRIBI · IVSSIT · A · DOM · MDCCCLVIII

CHAPTER 8

Does the Church Matter?

I believe in the Holy Spirit, the holy Christian Church, the communion of saints, the forgiveness of sins, the resurrection of the body, and the life everlasting. Amen. (Apostles' Creed)

And I believe in one holy Christian and apostolic Church, I acknowledge one Baptism for the remission of sins, and I look for the resurrection of the dead and the life of the world to come. Amen. (Nicene Creed)

Our churches teach that one holy Church is to remain forever. The Church is the congregation of saints [Psalm 149:1] *in which the Gospel is purely taught, and the Sacraments are correctly administered.*[60]

In our day and age, does the church really matter? Several years ago, there was a video making the rounds on social media that claimed Jesus is greater than religion. The whole premise of the popular video was that believing in Jesus was something higher than the church: a personal faith that exists in and unto itself. Though the video didn't quite phrase it that way, this was the message it conveyed. The video resonated well with many people because it

60 AC VII 1.

made them think that in the end, the church doesn't matter. What matters is simply what you believe and that you are in the driver's seat in this whole Christianity thing because after all, Jesus is greater than religion.

Though it shouldn't surprise us, we err when we fall into this line of thinking. Our old sinful nature, the devil, and the world want nothing more than for us to separate ourselves from Christ. If we can appear godly in the process, all the better. Indeed, our faith in Christ is personal. It is a gift of God through the means of grace. Yet the thing is, Christianity *is* a religion. That is the very nature of God's Word. The Holy Scriptures reveal God and what He says about Himself to us. We don't define the Christian faith; God reveals and gives it to us and teaches us what He would have us know.

Along those same lines is another sentiment pastors will often hear from people: "I don't need to go to church to be a Christian." Usually this is a response given by someone when confronted about not coming to church. It expresses the same line of thinking as the previous example from the popular video. The sentiment is that there's a disconnect in the world between Jesus and the Christian Church. In the minds of many in the public, it's as if the two are not inherently related. If this is so, the question, then, is, "Does the church matter?"

The Lutheran Confessions have a fair amount to say about the church. Maybe that's not surprising to you, or maybe it is. The Augsburg Confession was significant in church history, as it defined what the church is and how it is known. Melanchthon wrote, "Our churches teach that one holy Church is to remain forever. The Church is the congregation of saints [Psalm 149:1] in which the Gospel is purely taught, and the Sacraments are correctly administered." That's something important to think about as we consider the church and if it matters. The church is not a club or just an assembly of like-minded individuals. The church is the Bride of Christ.

God has given His church, this Bride of Christ, to us. Ephesians 5:25–30 gives us this beautiful image of the church. God inspired Paul to write,

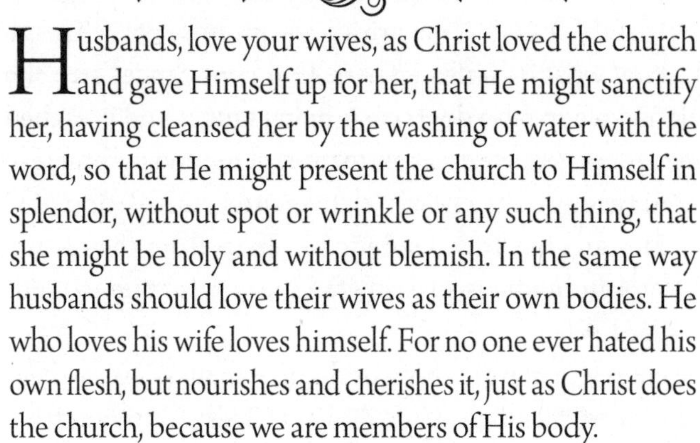

> Husbands, love your wives, as Christ loved the church and gave Himself up for her, that He might sanctify her, having cleansed her by the washing of water with the word, so that He might present the church to Himself in splendor, without spot or wrinkle or any such thing, that she might be holy and without blemish. In the same way husbands should love their wives as their own bodies. He who loves his wife loves himself. For no one ever hated his own flesh, but nourishes and cherishes it, just as Christ does the church, because we are members of His body.

Now, imagine if a bride, on her wedding day, made the claim that she doesn't need or want her husband. How would we respond to that line of thinking? It would seem preposterous to us! So it is when we claim that the church and Jesus do not need each other.

A document in the Lutheran Confessions that speaks a great deal about what the church is, and one that is often overlooked or lumped into another, is the Treatise on the Power and Primacy of the Pope (The Treatise sometimes has been considered an appendix to the Smalcald Articles, but it is helpful to see it for the document it is on its own). It addresses exactly what it says it does as it speaks to the issues and problems of the papacy. At its core, the Treatise shows how the church is not defined by a head in Rome (the pope), who claims to attach the power of salvation to his office. The Treatise also extols the truth of what the church is and why the Lord has given it to us. It admonishes us to guard what Scripture teaches about the church and not let false teachings tear us away from Christ.

A right understanding of false teaching is important to think about amid any discussion about the church. At one point in the

Treatise, Melanchthon speaks bluntly and warns us what happens when a false understanding of the church is promoted. "So they hide Christ's glory and rob consciences of firm consolation. They abolish true divine services (i.e., the exercises of faith struggling with <unbelief and> despair <concerning the promise of the Gospel>)."[61] Think about what is confessed here. Our consciences are robbed of consolation when false doctrine is being taught and preached. The church matters because doctrine matters. True and faithful teaching, delivered through the church, delivers the consolation of Christ as only He can give. Independent and apart from the community of believers, individuals so easily fall into a false understanding of God's Word.

The church matters in this world, and it matters for us, the people of God who are members of the Body of Christ. The church is where Christ and salvation are given out through the means of grace. The church is where Christ is found and gives His consolation of forgiveness, life, and salvation. Where Christ is, there are the means of grace. The church matters because Christ and His Word matter.

Luther preaches about the forgiveness of sins and the church in a sermon on the Apostles' Creed in 1528, not long before he writes the catechisms:

> **Then, in this Christian church, you have "the forgiveness of sins." This term includes baptism, consolation upon a deathbed, the sacrament of the altar, absolution, and all the comforting passages [of the gospel]. In this term are included all the ministrations through which the church forgives sins, especially where the gospel, not laws or traditions, is preached. Outside of this church and these sacraments and [ministrations] there is no sanctification.**[62]

61 Tr 44.

62 Luther, *Luther's Works*, vol. 51, *Sermons I*, eds. John W. Doberstein and Helmut T. Lehmann

The church is a place where Christ is present for our benefit. We live as God's people, His kingdom, in the church. In the explanation of the Second Article of the Creed in the Small Catechism, Luther writes,

> **He has redeemed me, a lost and condemned creature, purchased and won me from all sins, from death, and from the power of the devil. He did this not with gold or silver, but with His holy, precious blood and with His innocent suffering and death, so that I may be His own, live under Him in His kingdom, and serve Him in everlasting righteousness, innocence, and blessedness, just as He is risen from the dead, lives and reigns to all eternity. This is most certainly true.**[63]

God makes us holy and delivers salvation to us in the church through the means of grace. The Large Catechism is helpful, as it forms our thinking and how we understand why the church matters and how we confess why it matters in the world. Luther provides some helpful background about the Third Commandment. He explains the Sabbath in terms of the ceremonial law of the Old Testament and how we are to understand this commandment now in light of Christ. He places an importance and holiness inherent in God's Word. Relics or works do not make us holy. Rather, it is the Word of God. We are to hold His Word as a treasure. As Christians, this is what the Third Commandment is about: hearing and learning God's Word.

Luther puts forth some questions for us to consider and use as we confess the church in our lives:

(Philadelphia: Fortress Press, 1959), 167.

63 SC II.

So when someone asks you, "What is meant by the commandment: You shall sanctify the holy day?" Answer like this, "To sanctify the holy day is the same as to keep it holy." "But what is meant by keeping it holy?" "Nothing else than to be occupied with holy words, works, and life." For the day needs no sanctification for itself. It has been created holy in itself. But God desires the day to be holy to you. Therefore, it becomes holy or unholy because of you, whether you are occupied on that day with things that are holy or unholy.

How, then, does such sanctification take place? Not like this: sitting behind the stove and doing no rough work, or adorning ourselves with a wreath and putting on our best clothes. But as said above, we occupy ourselves with God's Word and exercise ourselves in the Word.[64]

Luther continues by conveying the importance of setting time aside for all Christians to participate in the Divine Service. In a day and age where everything is individualistic and private, the Christian faith is corporate and very public. God's people are made holy by the Word of God, and they gather together to hear and learn the Word preached to them. Luther also teaches us about the need for intentional retention of what has been handed down to us. From the beginning of the church, Christians gathered together on Sundays. Luther emphasizes that this is still the case. The Lutheran Church is not a sect but a continuation of the "catholic faith." This is the same faith confessed in the Three Ecumenical Creeds, and we continue to gather around it like the church has for centuries since the day

64 LC I 87–88.

of our Lord's resurrection. We set aside this day for the intentional reception of the means of grace together as God's people. Knowing this significance of the church calls us to examine our lives and repent where we have despised what God has instituted and gives.

Understanding where God is at work and who we are as the church, we don't just make attending church worship services a priority. Its importance goes way beyond that of a priority. The book of Acts describes the gathering of the church after the day of Pentecost in this way: "So those who received his word were baptized, and there were added that day about three thousand souls. And they devoted themselves to the apostles' teaching and the fellowship, to the breaking of bread and the prayers" (Acts 2:41–42). Notice that the people "devoted themselves." The Greek word translated as devoted here has meanings such as "stick to," "attach to," and "to be busy with something." That is what the people do in Acts 2:42. They devote themselves, stick to, attach themselves to, and are busy with the Word and Sacraments. Going to church and receiving the Word and Sacraments matters to them because they know why it is important. Their example teaches us what our attitude toward the church should be as well.

Being devoted to the things of God solidifies the importance of the church in our lives. In the Large Catechism, Luther exhorts, "Therefore, you must always have God's Word in your heart, upon your lips, and in your ears."[65] Driving home this point even further, we confess what the Large Catechism says in the article on the Lord's Supper when it teaches us to take the receiving of God's gifts seriously in our lives: "Now, it is true, as we have said, that no one should by any means be forced or compelled to go to the Sacrament, lest we institute a new murdering of souls. Nevertheless, it must be known that people who deprive themselves of and withdraw from the Sacrament for such a long time are not to be considered Christians."[66]

65 LC I 100.

66 LC V 42.

Finally, regarding what the church is and why it matters, the Large Catechism confesses the following in reference to the Third Article of the Apostles' Creed:

Everything, therefore, in the Christian Church is ordered toward this goal: we shall daily receive in the Church nothing but the forgiveness of sin through the Word and signs, to comfort and encourage our consciences as long as we live here. So even though we have sins, the <grace of the> Holy Spirit does not allow them to harm us. For we are in the Christian Church, where there is nothing but <continuous, uninterrupted> forgiveness of sin. This is because God forgives us and because we forgive, bear with, and help one another [Galatians 6:1–2].

But outside of this Christian Church, where the Gospel is not found, there is no forgiveness, as also there can be no holiness. Therefore, all who seek and wish to earn holiness not through the Gospel and forgiveness of sin, but by their works, have expelled and severed themselves <from this Church> [Galatians 5:4].[67]

Rejecting what God gives through the means of grace is both serious and detrimental to our eternal salvation. God calls us, then, to go where He is found. Within the church, we want to live out God's callings for us. It may sound obvious, but Christians should want Jesus and what He gives. The thing is, though, we are tempted to neglect, reject, or deny this.

The church matters. God calls us to faithfully know, confess, and live out this simple statement. God cares for us and gives great

67 LC II 55–56.

comfort to us through what Christ has done. The very fact that we are the church, the Body of Christ, and God has given us His Word and Sacraments, by which the Holy Spirit calls, gathers, enlightens, and sanctifies us, is a testament to the grace and love of God for us. God gives us our daily bread, but He also, and even more so, gives us the Bread of Life that came down from heaven. God forgives us, granting us life and salvation in His church through the means of grace. He has established a divine office in the church set apart for our benefit. The office of the holy ministry, the vocation of pastor, has been instituted by Christ Himself so that these means of grace are given to us. Matthew 28 and John 20 are two examples in the Gospels where Jesus establishes this office. The Lutheran Confessions confess this pastoral office of the ministry in many places, upholding it as a divinely instituted office given to the church for the benefit of God's people. The Lutheran Confessions confess this biblical truth in Articles V and XIV of the Augsburg Confession, among so many other places.

The church matters because we matter to God. He has purchased and won us with the price of the blood of Christ and has made us His own to live under Him in His kingdom forever. That reflects who we are as the Bride of Christ, the church, and how much the Lord treasures us.

This gets to another important truth the Lutheran Confessions confess: the church is eternal. That might sound odd at first, but it really is a comforting truth flowing from the promises of Christ. From the beginning of the Reformation and back throughout history, the church has been on peoples' minds. When we look around us, we see so many institutions that come and go. Even nations and great empires are here for a time on this earth and then are simply a thing of the past. The church is not a human institution. To be sure, there are buildings made with hands, but the eternal church of God is something far greater, and "the gates of hell shall prevail against it" (Matthew 16:18).

Does the church matter? The better questions are, "Does forgiveness matter?"; "Does life matter?"; "Does salvation matter?"; and "Does Christ matter?" The answer to those questions is, of course, yes! This is why the church matters and always will matter. In this confession, we see life within the church in relation to those who are outside of it. Inviting our family and neighbors to church is an invitation for them to see and meet Jesus. This confession takes the burden of thinking that somehow we can reason someone into the Christian faith off of us. Instead, much like what Jesus said to His first disciples, we, too, can say, "Come and you will see" (John 1:39). This is who we are and who we confess we are before the world. This is the longing we have for others to be part of this Body, the church. We desire for them to "see" and have Christ and His salvation, which are found in the church. The Smalcald Articles put it so beautifully when Luther writes about the Gospel: "God is superabundantly generous in His grace."[68] We confess this. We live it. We are Christ's Bride, the church. We are precious to Him now and forever.

QUESTIONS FOR FURTHER DISCUSSION AND STUDY:

1. Read the Smalcald Articles, Part III, Articles IV–VIII. In what ways do these articles help form how we understand that great consolation is found in the church through the means of grace?

2. The section in the Treatise on the Power and Primacy of the Pope where it ascribes the marks of the antichrist to the papacy often stirs up some controversy and discussion. Read the Treatise 39–59. Why do the Lutheran Confessions confess and teach this connection between the papacy and the antichrist? What is the purpose for confessing this connection as the church?

68 SA III IV.

CHAPTER 9

How Are God's People Known?

I believe that there is upon earth a little holy group and congregation of pure saints, under one head, even Christ [Ephesians 1:22]. This group is called together by the Holy Spirit in one faith, one mind, and understanding, with many different gifts, yet agreeing in love, without sects or schisms [Ephesians 4:5–8, 11]. I am also a part and member of this same group, a sharer and joint owner of all the goods it possesses [Romans 8:17]. I am brought to it and incorporated into it by the Holy Spirit through having heard and continuing to hear God's Word [Galatians 3:1–2], which is the beginning of entering it.[69]

How are God's people known? That question is critical as we consider the importance of being members of the church. God's people are holy people, the Bride and Body of Christ. They are saints as Ephesians 5:25–27 teaches us (along with other passages such as 1 Corinthians 1:2 and 2 Corinthians 1:1, to name a couple). God doesn't leave us wondering if we really are the church. He gives us marks to identify where His church is found.

69 LC II 51–52.

The writers of the Lutheran Confessions faced many issues when it came to how we understand what the church is, especially after those who adhered to Lutheran doctrines were excommunicated from the Roman Catholic Church. Rather than redefining the church on our own terms, it is important to let God's Word speak to us and confess what it means to be God's people.

Faith in Christ is what makes one a saint, and this happens by the work of the Holy Spirit. In this way, saints are a spiritual people. However, saints are known and found through external, outward things. This requires a little unpacking. As the Lutheran Confessions have already established in this book, the Holy Spirit works through the means of grace. This is not to say that as long as one simply has an official membership to a Christian congregation, one is still in the church. That's not the case. Salvation comes by grace through faith in Christ. Yet Christian congregations show us where God's people are found. It is in this outward thing, the physical gathering of God's people, where God's Word is faithfully preached and the Sacraments are administered according to the institution of Christ, where we find the church.

In the Apology of the Augsburg Confession, Melanchthon addresses where we find the church. He does so over and against those in the Roman Catholic Church who had tried to redefine the church as those who submit to the authority of the pope. He writes,

The Church is defined by the Third Article of the Creed, which teaches us to believe that there is a holy Catholic Church. The wicked indeed are not a holy Church. The words that follow, namely, "the communion of saints," seems to be added in order to explain what the Church signifies: the congregation of saints, who have with each other the fellowship of the same

Gospel or doctrine and the same Holy Spirit, who renews, sanctifies, and governs their hearts.[70]

The Third Article of the Apostles' Creed helps form how we think about where God's people are found. In many ways, what the church is and where the church is found are closely connected. In the Third Article, we confess, "I believe in the Holy Spirit, the holy Christian Church, the communion of saints, the forgiveness of sins, the resurrection of the body, and the life everlasting. Amen." Over the years, many theologians have been apt to point out how there is a double meaning to the phrase "the communion of saints." One way this phrase could be translated is the communion or fellowship of the *saints*. It could also be translated as the communion or fellowship of the *holy things*. The second translation understands the church to have a distinctive sacramental focus on who she is and what she does. God's people are known by where their Lord calls, gathers, enlightens, and sanctifies them through the means of grace.

This double meaning both encourages us to go where the church is and comforts us in knowing the author and sustainer of the church. In the Smalcald Articles, Luther makes a statement that is often quoted that gets to the heart of the meaning and purpose of the church. Luther writes, "Thank God, <today> a seven-year-old child knows what the Church is, namely, the holy believers and lambs who hear the voice of their Shepherd [John 10:11–16]. For the children pray, 'I believe in one holy Christian Church.'"[71] Saints are people who hear the voice of their Good Shepherd, Jesus. The primary place this happens is the church.

We are holy people living in a fallen world. Noah and his family on the ark show a picture of the church. We see how God keeps them safe and secure amid the flood as death surrounds them. That same Hebrew word for the ark is also used for the basket Moses was put

70 Ap VII and VIII 7–8.

71 SA III XII 2–3.

into to escape the killing of young boys in Egypt in the book of Exodus. It is no coincidence that many churches have an ark or nautical-shaped part of the building where the people sit in the pews. This part of the church is called the *nave* and is related to the word *navy*, which pertains to ships and the sea.

The Lutheran Confessions orient us saints to both see and know who we are as the church. In the explanation of the Third Petition of the Lord's Prayer, "Thy will be done on earth as it is in heaven," Luther preaches what God's people can expect as they seek to live faithfully: "But now arises a need that is just as great: we must firmly keep God's honor and our salvation, and not allow ourselves to be torn from them. . . . So in God's kingdom, although we have prayed for the greatest need—for the Gospel, faith, and the Holy Spirit, that He may govern us and redeem us from the devil's power—we must also pray that God's will be done. . . . We shall have to suffer many thrusts and blows on that account from everything that seeks to oppose and prevent the fulfillment of the first two petitions."[72]

Suffering is all around us in this world. Suffering for the sake of Christ and His Word is also a part of how God's people are known. Yet our suffering for the Gospel points us to the One who suffered for us on the cross. Luther addresses this in the Large Catechism: "If we would be Christians, therefore, we must surely expect and count on having the devil with all his angels and the world as our enemies [Matthew 25:41; Revelation 12:9]. They will bring every possible misfortune and grief upon us. For where God's Word is preached, accepted, or believed and produces fruit, there the holy cross cannot be missing [Acts 14:22]."[73]

Bearing the cross as the church is part of who we are as God's people. Notice, though, what brings this suffering about: the Word of God being preached and believed. Even as God's people see and experience suffering for the sake of the Gospel, God promises

72 LC III 60, 61.

73 LC III 65.

that He will deliver us and that His will will be done in our midst. Again, the Lutheran Confession teach about prayer in a way that focuses us back to God:

> **Such prayer, then, is to be our protection and defense now. It is to repel and put down all that the devil, pope, bishops, tyrants, and heretics can do against our Gospel. . . . Over and against this one or two Christians with this petition alone shall be our wall [Ezekiel 22:30], against which they shall run and dash themselves to pieces. We have this comfort and confidence: the devil's will and purpose and all our enemies shall and must fail and come to nothing, no matter how proud, secure, and powerful they know themselves to be. For if their will were not broken and hindered, God's kingdom could not remain on earth nor His name be hallowed.**[74]

During these attacks and assaults of the devil, which produce suffering, God drives His people back to the consolation of His Word and Sacraments. It doesn't have to be persecution that drives us back to God's Word. It can also be other forms of suffering and trial. For example, when I served in Iowa, something happened that brought this doctrine of the church to a head for me and all of the saints in that congregation. It drove us back to what defines us as the church, where the church is found, and how God will always take care of us as His people through His means of grace.

The year 2020 will never be forgotten by those who lived through it. It brings back memories of a pandemic, to be sure, but something else happened that caused both my congregation and me to go running back to what God's Word teaches us about who we are

74 LC III 69, 70.

as the church. The Lutheran Confessions played a vital role in our confession of Christ and formed how we endured a time of great trial and suffering.

It was the day after my second-oldest daughter's birthday when a derecho hit our town. It was a Monday, right around lunchtime. The previous day was Sunday, the Ninth Sunday after Trinity in the Church Year. That Sunday has appointed Luke 16:1–9 (10–13) as the Holy Gospel, the parable of the dishonest manager. The Hymn of Day is typically "What Is the World to Me" (*LSB* 730). My sermon that Sunday morning ended that with me saying, "Dear Christians, behold Jesus and ask, 'What is the world to me?' See your possessions, your time, your money, and all of the stuff in this world for what they truly are and who they are to serve rather than you serve them. Use them wisely not for evil but for good, for you are the sons of light called out of the darkness by the light of world. Be wise in these things and learn the example of shrewdness from those in this world and what great lengths they go to to preserve these institutions and possessions. Your heart, though, is where your Lord and His gifts are found. You see these things of this world for what they rightfully are and use them as those who belong to Christ and whose lives are lived in service to Him. As a fruit of your faith, you use mammon in service to Christ and His church and you teach your children to do the same. Your God isn't made with the hands of men but the one who has redeemed you by His blood. He is the one who gave up everything for your sake, for you are His treasure now and forever."

Then the next day came, and with it a storm that brought near 120-miles-per-hour winds for a sustained thirty minutes. When the storm hit, my family and I were in our basement. We could hear crashing all around us. We could hear sheer power and destruction ripping through our community.

After the storm seemed to calm, I went up and looked outside. We lived in the parsonage next door, and I saw the church building. I will forever remember that image, as it has been seared into my mind. A large portion of the church's roof had been ripped open like a banana peel, and there was debris everywhere. Inside the church, water was pouring in on the beautiful sanctuary and creating even more damage.

The small town we lived in was devastated. Homes and farms were destroyed. Everyone was affected by this storm. The days following it were a blur of visiting people and talking to various organizations. I remember the next day. I was sitting by myself in my study. I opened my hymnal and sang "From God Can Nothing Move Me" (*LSB* 713) as I tried to take in everything that was happening. That week, I prayed with people, hugged them, and listened to so many stories. I witnessed so many sights that will forever be etched in my memory. I heard "Why did this happen?" and "What do we do now?" There seemed to be more questions than answers.

Throughout that week, the lay leaders of the church and I met, trying to decide what to do next. What was never once even hinted at was canceling church services. We all knew that what we needed was what only God through His Word could give. We needed Christ. We decided that the coming Sunday we would set up folding chairs in an open space next to our devastated building. We wheeled out hymnals on a cart. We set up a makeshift altar. We hooked up a portable speaker to a generator and gathered right there in that place to hear the Word of God together as the church.

Just one week later, over the loud hum of a generator, I proclaimed in my sermon, "Last week seems like so long ago, but Jesus Christ is the same yesterday, today, and forever. We sang the hymn 'What Is the World to Me' last week and heard about not loving the things of the world over God and using the things of this world in service to God with no idea what the week would hold and what a trial would be in store for us. But on this Sunday, the same words ring true in a perhaps starker way. We sit here this morning and cling to Christ's promises, lacking more in a worldly sense than we did a week ago but still possessing the Lord and His kingdom. Your confession is still the same as the Lord is the same Lord for you who is your treasure. 'What is the world to me with all its vaunted pleasure when You, and You alone, Lord Jesus, are my treasure! You only, dearest Lord, my soul's delight shall be; You are my peace, my rest. What is the world to me!'"[75]

The weeks and months went by, and God's people rebuilt the church building and loved one another. Another congregation in our circuit offered to let us use their building for services while the new church building was being constructed, and they welcomed us into their midst as brothers and sisters in Christ. Finally, after so much labor and waiting, everything was brought to a resolution, and God's people were once again back in the restored church building.

As we think about this example and where God's people are known, we find consolation in Christ. The Augsburg Confession rightly confesses, "Our churches teach that one holy Church is to remain forever. The Church is the congregation of saints [Psalm 149:1] in which the Gospel is purely taught and the Sacraments are correctly administered."[76] This truth formed how our congregation understood who we were and where we were known after the devastating storm hit. We knew our building couldn't be used again, but that didn't change who we were as a congregation. To be sure, it is important to have a place set apart for people to gather around the things of God. What defined us as a congregation of God's people, though, were God's Word and Sacraments. Nothing could take God's promises away from us.

Likewise, knowing where God is found for us in His means of grace, we know the importance of gathering to receive God's gifts even when there are hundreds of other things that can take our time and attention. God's people receive God's gifts. That's who they are as His saints and where they are found.

No matter what situation in life we may be facing, God's people will always be God's people who are known by the means God has

---

75 *LSB* 730:1.

76 AC VII 1.

appointed. Think about the church of God and our confession of Christ in the world. This is the confidence we have that withstands anything and is unchanging no matter what situation we may face. We are God's saints, and He will guard and keep us as His people. We fix our eyes on Christ, who is our Head, and receive from His gracious hands the unchanging and unwavering salvation He has accomplished for us.

QUESTIONS FOR FURTHER DISCUSSION AND STUDY:

1. Read the Apology of the Augsburg Confession, Articles VII and VIII. Melanchthon brings up some other topics pertaining to what the church is and how God's people are known. What are some of these things? What consolation in Christ is proclaimed as it relates to the church in these articles?
2. Go back to the statement of Luther quoted in the chapter from the Smalcald Articles (SA III XII) about a child knowing what the church is and think about it. How does this help form our thinking about God's people being known and confessing that in the world?

FRIDERICVS · GVILELMVS · IV · REX · PORTAM [illegible] QVA · MARTINVS · LVTHERVS · A · DOM · MDXVII
[illegible] OCTOBR · D · XXXI · INDVLGENTIIS · ROMANIS [illegible] IMPVGNANDIS · THESES · AFFIXIT · LXXXXV
REFORMATIONIS · SACRORVM · PRAENVNTIAS [illegible] INCENDIO · VASTATAM · REFECIT · SIGNIS · EXORNAVIT
VALVAS · EX · AERE · FIERI · ATQVE · ILLAS · THESES [illegible] INSCRIBI · IVSSIT · A · DOM · MDCCCLVII

CHAPTER 10

What Does the World Need?

And what need is there for more words? If I were to list all the profit and fruit God's Word produces, where would I get enough paper and time? The devil is called the master of a thousand arts. But what shall we call God's Word, which drives away and brings to nothing this master of a thousand arts with all his arts and power? The Word must indeed be the master of more than a hundred thousand arts. And shall we easily despise such power, profit, strength, and fruit—we, especially, who claim to be pastors and preachers? If so, not only should we have nothing given us to eat, but we should also be driven out, baited with dogs, and pelted with dung. We not only need all this every day just as we need our daily bread, but we must also daily use it against the daily and unending attacks and lurking of the devil [1 Peter 5:8], the master of a thousand arts.[77]

77 LC Preface 12–13.

What does the world need? The short answer to that question is, of course, Jesus. Everyone, in every place and at every time, needs Jesus. We need Him in times of joy and sadness. We need Him in times of lack and plenty. We need Him in times of life and death. There is never any moment where we don't need Jesus, what He has accomplished for us, and what He gives to us.

There's a reason, then, why we make a big deal about faithfully confessing the Christian faith in the world. God's Word is our treasure and the instrument through which God accomplishes His purposes. God's Word is active, and Christians should desire this Word to be among us in all aspects of our lives. This is nothing new.

The devil, the world, and our sinful flesh create traps for us when it comes to the desire to apply God's Word. There's always a temptation for us to approach reading the Lutheran Confessions like a history book that has no relevancy for today. Hopefully, by reading this book, that temptation has been overcome. Unfortunately, we are also tempted to approach the Bible in the same way, as if the historical contexts distance us from applicability. God's Word, though, is the truth, and this has no time stamp. This is the same when it comes to confessing this truth of the central teachings of Holy Scriptures as laid out in the Lutheran Confessions. The Lutheran Confessions were written long ago, but they speak to today just as much as they spoke to the issues facing their writers. The issues might not always be a one-to-one correlation, but the need of Christ and the call of God to confess this faith are the same.

The Prefaces to the Small and Large Catechisms are particularly helpful for us to see how even then, just as now, the world needed Jesus. Prior to writing and publishing the catechisms, Luther had been asked by his ruler, Frederick, to help serve as a visitor for the churches in the region. These visitations assessed the state of the churches. Among other things, they revealed an abysmal catechesis not just of the people but also of the pastors. In response, Luther preached a series of sermons on various topics such as the Ten Commandments, the Creed, and the Lord's Prayer, which were the primary texts addressed by catechisms of the day. He also preached on topics pertaining to the Sacraments. These series of catechetical sermons in 1528 formed the basis, both in content and language, of what eventually became the Large Catechism. Luther then wrote the Large and Small Catechisms in 1529.

The Preface to the Small Catechism references some of the lack of understanding of the Christian faith in these churches. Luther does not sugarcoat what he witnessed going on in the churches:

> **The deplorable, miserable condition that I discovered recently when I, too, was a visitor, has forced and urged me to prepare this catechism, or Christian doctrine, in this small, plain, simple form. Mercy! Dear God, what great misery I beheld! The common person, especially in the villages, has no knowledge whatever of Christian doctrine. And unfortunately, many pastors are completely unable and unqualified to teach. <This is so much so, that one is ashamed to speak of it.> Yet, everyone says that they are Christians, have been baptized, and receive the holy Sacraments, even though they cannot even recite the Lord's Prayer or the Creed or the Ten Commandments. They live like dumb brutes and irrational hogs. Now that the Gospel has come, they have nicely learned to abuse all freedom like experts.**[78]

The people needed to be taught the things of God. Could the same be said of the world we live in today? How about the church? We are always in need of Christ and always in need of ongoing instruction in God's Word. Luther used the catechisms as something to help

78 SC Preface 1–3.

us do this, not for the sake of his own self-promotion but because of how the catechisms summarize and confess the Christian faith. The catechisms help form our confession of faith as well so that we can faithfully confess Christ to world around us.

In the Preface to the Large Catechism, Luther writes about God's Word,

> **We not only need all this every day just as we need our daily bread, but we must also daily use it against the daily and unending attacks and lurking of the devil [1 Peter 5:8], the master of a thousand arts.**
>
> **If these reasons were not enough to move us to read the catechism daily, we should feel bound well enough by God's command alone. He solemnly commands in Deuteronomy 6:6–8 that we should always meditate on His precepts, sitting, walking, standing, lying down, and rising. We should have them before our eyes and in our hands as a constant mark and sign. Clearly He did not solemnly require and command this without a purpose. For He knows our danger and need, as well as the constant and furious assaults and temptations of devils. He wants to warn, equip, and preserve us against them, as with a good armor against their fiery darts [Ephesians 6:10–17] and with good medicine against their evil infection and temptation.**[79]

We need the Word of God. The world needs the Word of God. God forms our confession of Christ and His Word. This formation starts with us being students of the Word but continues as our very existence as God's people daily studying and meditating upon it.

79 LC Preface 13–14.

Our confession of Christ will only be made stronger as we see our need for Christ and His Word, daily listening to our Lord.

The Formula of Concord echoes the importance of God's Word being our teacher: "After God (through the Holy Spirit in Baptism) has kindled and caused a beginning of the true knowledge of God and faith, we should pray to Him without ceasing [1 Thessalonians 5:17]. We should ask that through the same Spirit and His grace, by means of the daily exercise of reading and doing God's Word, He would preserve in us faith and His heavenly gifts, strengthen us from day to day, and keep us to the end. For unless God Himself is our schoolmaster, we can study and learn nothing that is acceptable to Him and helpful to ourselves and others."[80]

Preaching on the Second Petition, "Thy kingdom come," Luther teaches this truth of how God hears and answers our prayers and how His Word works in this world. He writes,

We pray here in the first place that this may happen with us. We pray that His name may be so praised through God's holy Word and a Christian life that we who have accepted it may abide and daily grow in it, and that it may gain approval and acceptance among other people. We pray that it may go forth with power throughout the world [2 Thessalonians 3:1]. We pray that many may find entrance into the kingdom of grace [John 3:5], be made partakers of redemption [Colossians 1:12–14], and be led to it by the Holy Spirit [Romans 8:14], so that we may all together remain forever in the one kingdom now begun.

For the coming of God's kingdom to us happens in two ways: (a) here in time through the Word and faith [Matthew 13]; and (b) in eternity forever

80 FC SD II 16.

> **through revelation [Luke 19:11; 1 Peter 1:4–5]. Now we pray for both these things. We pray that the kingdom may come to those who are not yet in it, and, by daily growth that it may come to us who have received it, both now and hereafter in eternal life. All this is nothing other than saying, "Dear Father, we pray, give us first Your Word, so that the Gospel may be preached properly throughout the world. Second, may the Gospel be received in faith and work and live in us, so that through the Word and the Holy Spirit's power [Romans 15:18–19], Your kingdom may triumph among us. And we pray that the devil's kingdom be put down [Luke 11:17–20], so that he may have no right or power over us [Luke 10:17–19; Colossians 1], until at last his power may be utterly destroyed. So sin, death, and hell shall be exterminated [Revelation 20:13–14]. Then we may live forever in perfect righteousness and blessedness" [Ephesians 4:12–13].**[81]

When we pray for God's kingdom to come or His will to be done, we confess that both we and the world around us need Christ and His Word. We trust the promises of God that He hears and answers our prayers on account of Christ. This prayer gives us confidence in knowing who our Father is and how He will hear us, answer us, and take care of us, His dear children.

Jesus is the light of world. As His people, the church confesses Christ as the light shining in the darkness of the fallen the world. We the church are a city that God has set on a hill. Yet our light is not dependent upon us, nor are we left lacking in what our Lord would have us say. We have His Word, the Holy Scriptures, which means we have everything. Confessing Christ leads us to Christ

81 LC III 52–54.

Himself. Trusting the Word of God comforts us and gives peace to our consciences. Even when everything around us seems to be against us, we always remember that we both need and have Christ.

QUESTIONS FOR FURTHER STUDY AND DISCUSSION:

1. How does the Lord's Prayer help us see and understand the world around us, what it needs, and how God gives us what we need in Christ?
2. How does being diligent about being students of the Word of God help us not only form our confession of Christ but want to do so in the world?

CHAPTER 11

"Who Do You Say That I Am?"

This is the catholic faith; whoever does not believe it faithfully and firmly cannot be saved. (Athanasian Creed)

"Who do you say that I am?" We come back to the question we explored in chapter 1 as we looked at the confession of Peter in Matthew 16. Although it is drastically declining, there is still a sense that Christianity is part of the American culture. What this means is another thing. For the most part, many people we come in contact with daily have had at least some exposure or some familiarity with Christianity. This is changing, though, and the opportunities to confess the Christian faith to those outside of it are increasing.

Let's think about another scenario that could occur (and has occurred for me personally) and how this concept of thinking confessionally helps us confess Christ and His Word in our lives. The scenario takes place in a small midwestern town in a public setting or get-together. At a meal for a relative who is a member of the congregation, an individual sees the pastor in his clerical collar and finds an opportunity to confront him. The pastor, trying to be friendly, introduces himself to this person. Very early into this conversation, however, the man brazenly asks, "Why are you Christians telling me what to think and do?" This question, or any variation of it, is indicative of the current American culture. The emphasis is on personal choices and freedoms of the individual. The idea of a religious group imposing its views and beliefs on others is offensive. The individual in the scenario is someone who could come from any number of backgrounds or age brackets within the culture.

The interesting thing about an individual who may bring up a question like this is he may have even been exposed to the Christian faith. Though he could have grown up with no connection to Christianity, he could also have grown up in an environment with some exposure to the faith but abandoned this for a more independent view of his life. He easily could have some sort of chip on his shoulder or grudge against the church and God's people for one reason or another. His thinking, whatever the case, is directed against the Christian faith.

There are certain assumptions that typically underlie this way of thinking. It's always helpful for us to consider what is specifically being said. In this scenario, one major idea is that we are free regarding the things of God. This mindset gets agitated when it hears something claiming objectivity and universality about truth that challenges its way of thinking. It assumes we are free to do whatever we like in life, and it does not want to have to answer something or someone outside of itself. In terms of the Christian faith, this false view sees itself free in relation to both God's Law and His Gospel. In terms of the Law, the person with this mindset sees God as the oppressor of people and that God's Law constricts and controls people from truly living a life of fulfillment and joy. Freedom becomes defined in terms of autonomy or subjective standards as is summarized well at the end of the book of Judges: "In those days there was no king in Israel. Everyone did what was right in his own eyes" (Judges 21:25).

Another assumption that applies to the individual in this scenario concerns both the human will when it comes to believing in God and a view of the Christian life. It thinks one is free to choose to follow Jesus or simply be neutral toward Him. This mindset betrays an indifference toward the things of God that manifests itself in a life that might not be hostile to God yet has an attitude that amounts to an almost spiritual libertarianism, so to speak. It believes that as long as no one forces some religious standard upon another person, religion has a right to exist in culture.

Much of what passes for religion today, then, is an individualistic understanding that sees no connection among man, God, and the church. To find the view of the person in the above scenario, one would not have to search very hard. The person catechized in this sort of thinking would have no doubt been taught this simply by his exposure to the current climate of conversation about religion found in public schools, universities, and in the public discourse.

We return to that question Jesus asks Peter in Matthew 16: "But who do you say that I am?" Christians give answer to that question in our lives as the church, the people of God whom the Holy Spirit has called, gathered, enlightened, and sanctified. As we have been studying, Lutherans have this work of the Holy Spirit in mind. They show us the cohesiveness of Christian doctrine and how it's all connected. Confessing the faith is what the whole church of Christ does. The Confessions, in the prefaces to many of the documents, make this point very clear: We confess Christ and His doctrine, and we are not alone in this task. The faithful cloud of witnesses who have gone before us and handed down this confession give us consolation. We give answer with them by repeating their confession in this same church.

Another interesting point of background to the Lutheran Confessions is the role that laymen played in both individual documents and the Book of Concord. Melanchthon is a prime example of this; he wrote the Augsburg Confession, the Apology of the Augsburg Confession, and the Treatise on the Power and Primacy of the Pope. Melanchthon was a scholar and theologian, to be sure, but he was not a pastor. He was giving answer to "Who do you say that I am?" from what God's Word, the Scriptures, say. He was confessing the faith, and the whole church was confessing along with him.

Other laymen signed their names to the documents. They subscribed to them and boldly stood up to princes, emperors, and popes. Psalm 119:46 says, "I will also speak of Your testimonies before kings and shall not be put to shame." This is exactly what so many Christian laymen have done since as they confessed this faith that has been handed down to them in the Lutheran Confessions. Various other rulers also saw to things like the printing of these documents and protecting faithful preachers and congregations who confessed the truth, without regard for the worldly cost and suffering such actions might bring to themselves. Giving answer before God and the world is what the church does. The church confesses Christ and His Word. We have God-given roles and duties and don't try to abolish or downplay these distinctions. The point, however, is that Christian laymen and pastors confess the faith.

As Christians, God calls both pastors and laymen to give answer to those who question us about the Christian faith. There isn't always time to say, "Let me research this and get back to you" (although some questions require that response). Two Bible passages come to mind for the people of God in general and pastors in particular. In 1 Peter 3:14–15, Peter writes, "But even if you should suffer for righteousness' sake, you will be blessed. Have no fear of them, nor be troubled, but in your hearts honor Christ the Lord as holy, always being prepared to make a defense to anyone who asks you for a reason for the hope that is in you; yet do it with gentleness and respect." This is for all people. For pastors in particular, there is a charge given to them by God in 2 Timothy 4:1–2: "I charge you in the presence of God and of Christ Jesus, who is to judge the living and the dead, and by His appearing and His kingdom: preach the word; be ready in season and out of season; reprove, rebuke, and exhort, with complete patience and teaching."

The task of giving answer, then, comes from a grounded, orthodox confession of God's Word. This is why it is of utmost importance that God's people be diligent in the study of the Scriptures, not only to faithfully confess the truth but for the Spirit's ongoing nurture of our own souls. Likewise, we study the Lutheran Confessions because they agree with the Scriptures. Our study not only gives us the knowledge to answer the questions asked of us by an unbelieving world, but it forms our thinking in how we are to go about daily living this confession.

Using this scenario of the individual mentioned above, the Christian can use the Lutheran Confessions in ways that can help form the pastor's thinking and response. The pastor could ask himself, "Who or what is this person's god?" The pastor could recall the First Commandment, which helps us consider what someone fears, loves, and trusts about his god. The pastor could also ask himself, "Why is he asking this question?" This helps the pastor recall how the individual's question is connected with how one understands the very nature of the Christian faith or Christ Himself. This second question will give clues to the man's overall mindset about Christ and His church.

A student and confessor of the confessions prepares to answer accusing questions from an unbeliever by first considering the doctrine of man and who this person is before responding. A central thing to keep in mind for the pastor or layperson in any discussion is man's bound will. This seemingly obvious fact, for Lutherans at least, is always a good starting point when dealing with someone outside of the faith. It is important, as one sees the old man, our sinful nature, continually rear his head in the life of the Christian. The language and thought of the Formula of Concord is helpful:

First, mankind's reason or natural intellect does still have a dim spark of the knowledge that there is a God. It also knows about the doctrine of the Law (Romans 1:19–21, 24, 32). Yet it is so ignorant, blind, and perverted that even when the most ingenious and learned people on earth read or hear the Gospel of God's Son and the promise of eternal salvation, they cannot by

> **their own powers perceive, apprehend, understand, or believe and regard it as true. They want to understand these spiritual things with their reason. But the more diligently and seriously they try, the less they understand or believe. Before they become enlightened and are taught by the Holy Spirit, they regard all this only as foolishness or fictions.**[82]

It is tempting for a Christian to think she can somehow outsmart someone outside the faith or use her intellect and rhetoric to somehow convince or win him over. The strong language the article from the Solid Declaration is a reminder of who man is. The fact that all humans are sinners should always be in the background of the minds of Christians who are called upon to confess their faith, to humble them and place God's Word at the center of their confession, with the Holy Spirit as the actor who teaches even as He calls, gathers, enlightens, and sanctifies.

As we recall the scenario at the beginning of this chapter, we are wise to remember that the evangelization task is ultimately in the hands of God. This truth takes the burden off the Christian in this situation as he confesses the faith to his neighbor. We engage the person with a mindset that isn't one of forcing but rather presenting God's truth to someone who is dying and has turned against God. It is not a battle of the wills but a proclamation of the victory already won in Christ. It is a confession of this hope that has been revealed to us by the Holy Scriptures.

Whether a conversation like the scenario in this chapter involves an ongoing exchange of questions and answers will vary from person to person, but the main point is that there is an engaging conversation, however brief it may be. This will address the question "Why are you telling me what to do?" from a perspective that has examined life in general and brought it back to him through

82 FC SD II 9.

the lens of God's Word. Though biases and assumptions might be revealed and can be addressed if needed, the goal is repentance and faith for the unbeliever.

One approach in the scenario would be for the pastor to bring up life in general. He could talk about how there are so many things we see around us that we are enslaved to and how this bondage becomes overwhelming as we are being tossed from one thing to another. We abuse and worship the things of the world instead of the Creator. Luther vividly shows similar thinking and explanation in the Large Catechism:

> **For if we believed this teaching with the heart, we would also act according to it [James 2:14]. We would not strut about proudly, act defiantly, and boast as though we had life, riches, power, honor, and such, of ourselves [James 4:13–16]. We would not act as though others must fear and serve us, as is the practice of the wretched, perverse world. The world is drowned in blindness and abuses all the good things and God's gifts only for its own pride, greed, lust, and luxury. It never once thinks about God, so as to thank Him or acknowledge Him as Lord and Creator.**[83]

This is especially helpful in a small-town midwestern mindset that sees itself as independent and hard-working. While true in some sense, no one is truly autonomous, and this is especially the case when it comes to God. It is important to get this line of thought going in a discussion when talking with someone who sees the Christian faith as intrusive or downright hostile. We are to point the person to sin and what the fallen world is and how, apart from Christ, we

83 LC II 21.

are slave to these things in the world and ourselves. This confession by the pastor or any Christian is essential.

Other documents in the Confessions such as the Creed or the Augsburg Confession provide further organization and content to a dialogue with an unbeliever. For example, the structure of the Creed presents first who we are as creatures of God, then redemption in Christ, and then the faith worked by the Holy Spirit through the means of grace. Thinking through this order and organization helps Christians work through a discussion while not losing sight of how God operates. Something similar could be said of the first five articles of the Augsburg Confession. The Lutheran Confessions are normed by God's Word and serve God's people well in so many ways. As our investigation of the opening scenario shows, the Lutheran Confessions help us give faithful answers to those who question the Christian faith. In such a dialogue, the door has been opened for a proclamation of the Gospel as what it truly means to be free.

Within this scenario, the pastor in a short amount of time has worked through the doctrine of original sin and proclaimed it to this man. Now he preaches the Gospel to him. The Creed (along with countless other articles throughout the Confessions) can provide a great way of summarizing and presenting the Gospel. It is as if Luther has this idea of a dialogue in mind when he comments in the Large Catechism,

> **Now, if you are asked, "What do you believe in the Second Article about Jesus Christ?" answer briefly, "I believe that Jesus Christ, God's true Son, has become my Lord."**
>
> **"But what does it mean to become Lord?"**
>
> **"It is this. He has redeemed me from sin, from the devil, from death, and from all evil. For before I did not have a Lord or King, but was captive under the**

devil's power, condemned to death, stuck in sin and blindness" [see Ephesians 2:1–3].

For when we had been created by God the Father and had received from Him all kinds of good, the devil came and led us into disobedience, sin, death, and all evil [Genesis 3]. So we fell under God's wrath and displeasure and were doomed to eternal damnation, just as we had merited and deserved. There was no counsel, help, or comfort until this only and eternal Son of God—in His immeasurable goodness—had compassion upon our misery and wretchedness. He came from heaven to help us [John 1:9]. So those tyrants and jailers are all expelled now. In their place has come Jesus Christ, Lord of life, righteousness, every blessing, and salvation. He has delivered us poor, lost people from hell's jaws, has won us, has made us free [Romans 8:1–2], and has brought us again into the Father's favor and grace. He has taken us as His own property under His shelter and protection [Psalm 61:3–4] so that He may govern us by His righteousness, wisdom, power, life, and blessedness.[84]

True freedom, life, and salvation is found only in Christ. This is what it means that Jesus is our Lord—He has redeemed us from sin, death, and the devil. God works a miracle over and against our old man when we believe the Gospel. Hearts, minds, and wills are changed by the Holy Spirit, and we no longer stand as God's enemies. It truly is a wonderful and freeing thing to have this precious gift of God here and unto life everlasting.

The individual who asked the accusing question in this scenario would, no doubt, have others and will most likely still need to talk

84 LC II 27–30.

more. This is but one small yet important element in an ongoing dialogue. Other topics need to be addressed in due time, but in the context of a dinner or social function when a pastor or another Christian has a limited amount of time, this framework established by the Lutheran Confessions is what he should focus on.

The Lutheran Confessions confess and teach the Holy Scriptures. Rightly confessing the faith to one's neighbor is daunting, yet the Confessions provide a roadmap to navigate this task, not only in their content but in how they thoughtfully approach sensitive topics. The Lutheran Confessions aid Christians in this task they are called to as they live out their lives in faith toward God and in love toward their neighbors.

A student of the Lutheran Confessions is one who knows calling, and the Confessions form his whole understanding and approach to both his own Christian faith and the role he serves in this fallen world. The writers of the Formula of Concord lived in a different time and culture than the situation presented here, but the Christian faith transcends time and culture. The Holy Spirit, through the means of grace, comes into time and creates a new culture: the culture of redemption and the Holy Christian Church. It is truly catholic in its confession. The issues confronted in the Lutheran Confessions remain the same as sin is still in the world and Jesus is still the only true Redeemer. May God grant His church faithfulness in our present time and in the future until He comes again in glory. The boldness to confess the faith comes from the Holy Spirit Himself, and with the writers of the Formula of Concord, we pray our witness may be faithful.

The end of the Solid Declaration teaches and encourages us:

In the sight of God and of all Christendom <the entire Church of Christ>, we want to testify to those now living and those who will come after us. This declaration presented here about all the controverted articles mentioned and explained above—and no other—is our faith, doctrine, and confession. By God's grace, with intrepid hearts, we are willing to appear before the judgment seat of Christ with this Confession and give an account of it [1 Peter 4:5]. We will not speak or write anything contrary to this Confession, either publicly or privately. By the strength of God's grace we intend to abide by it. Therefore, after mature deliberation, we have, in the fear of God and by calling on His name, attached our signatures with our own hands.[85]

Thanks be to God for such a confession in the documents of the Lutheran Confessions. The Christian faith does and must confess Christ as Peter answers when Jesus asks in Matthew 16, "Who do you say that I am?" The Creeds and the Lutheran Confessions will always exist even if man tries to reject them. The Lutheran Confessions provide a faithful witness to the Christian faith in whatever situation we made find ourselves in as we walk through this fallen world as ones who have been redeemed and marked in Holy Baptism by Christ, the crucified.

---

85 FC SD XII 40.

QUESTIONS FOR FURTHER DISCUSSION AND STUDY:

1. Why is it important for us to be confident in confessing Christ?
2. Read the Preface directed to Emperor Charles V at the beginning of the Augsburg Confession. How can we learn from the example of those men who presented the Augsburg Confession? What confidence did they have to confess the faith before the Holy Roman Emperor?

[illegible]RIDERICUS GUILELMUS IV REX PORTA[illegible] [illegible] QUA MARTINUS LUTHERUS A. DOM. MDXVII
[illegible] OCTOBR. D. XXXI INDULGENTIIS ROMAN[illegible] [illegible]MPUGNANDIS THESES AFFIXIT LXXXX[illegible]
[illegible]EFORMATIONIS SACRORUM PRAENUNTIAS [illegible] [illegible]CENDIO VASTATAM REFECIT SIGNIS EXORNAVIT
VALVAS [illegible] ATQUE ILLAS THES[illegible] [illegible]SCRIBI JUSSIT A. DOM. MDCCCLVII

CHAPTER 12

What Does the Future Look like for Us?

Our churches teach that at the end of the world Christ will appear for judgment and will raise all the dead [1 Thessalonians 4:13–5:2]. He will give the godly and elect eternal life and everlasting joys, but He will condemn ungodly people and the devils to be tormented without end [Matthew 25:31–46].

Our churches condemn the Anabaptists, who think that there will be an end to the punishments of condemned men and devils.

Our churches also condemn those who are spreading certain Jewish opinions, that before the resurrection of the dead the godly shall take possession of the kingdom of the world, the ungodly being everywhere suppressed.[86]

What does the future look like for us? The future can seem terrifying because it's unknown, or at least we think it's unknown. Sure, there are certain things that we don't know about the future, like who will win the World Series next year, who will

86 AC XVII 1–5.

win the next election, and how many cars I will own in my lifetime. On a more serious note, we don't know how long we will live on this earth. These things are unknown as we go through this life. Yet even with all that is unknown, we Christians know the ultimate future. In fact, the future is something that is not only known to us, but it is a sure and certain thing. As Christians, we know what our future will hold, which gives us confidence and consolation here and now.

The Holy Scriptures proclaim this to us time and again. In Matthew 24 (along with other topics like His death and the destruction of Jerusalem), Jesus speaks about His second coming. He says, "Then will appear in heaven the sign of the Son of Man, and then all the tribes of the earth will mourn, and they will see the Son of Man coming on the clouds of heaven with power and great glory. And He will send out His angels with a loud trumpet call, and they will gather His elect from the four winds, from one end of heaven to the other" (vv. 30–31). Jesus tells us that He is indeed coming again. We hear this in numerous readings every year in church at the end of the Church Year and during the season of Advent, which is derived from the Greek word for "coming."

The coming of Jesus on the Last Day is a sure and certain thing. It's not a matter of *if* it will happen but *when*. The when is known only to God, and that's fine. He is good and gracious, and we know that all things are in His hands. The Christian hope is one that knows what is coming or rather who is coming and why. Jesus is our Lord, and He comes for us to take us to be with Him and all His saints.

In Luke's Gospel, Jesus also mentions something to us about His coming. In Luke 21:25–33, Jesus says,

"And there will be signs in sun and moon and stars, and on the earth distress of nations in perplexity because of the roaring of the sea and the waves, people fainting with fear and with foreboding of what is coming on the world. For the powers of the

heavens will be shaken. And then they will see the Son of Man coming in a cloud with power and great glory. Now when these things begin to take place, straighten up and raise your heads, because your redemption is drawing near."

And He told them a parable: "Look at the fig tree, and all the trees. As soon as they come out in leaf, you see for yourselves and know that the summer is already near. So also, when you see these things taking place, you know that the kingdom of God is near. Truly, I say to you, this generation will not pass away until all has taken place. Heaven and earth will pass away, but My words will not pass away."

Jesus promises He is coming again in glory. He promises us that as we go through these last days (the time from His ascension until He returns), our redemption is drawing near. In all this, He promises us that His words will not pass away.

A great example of other places in Scripture that reveal our future is the great resurrection chapter of 1 Corinthians 15. There, God inspires Paul to beautifully lay before us what our future holds. In 1 Corinthians 15:51–56, he writes:

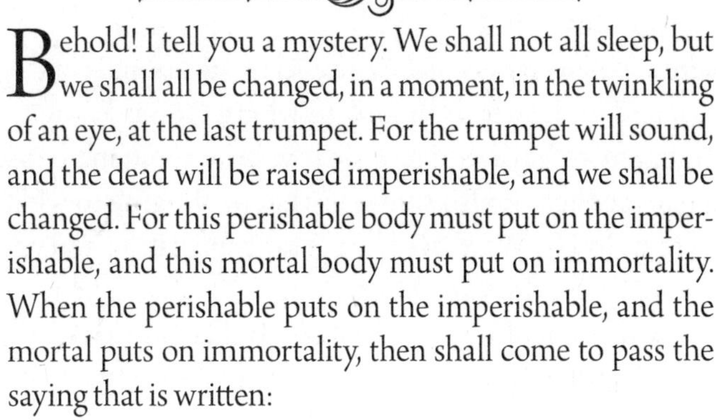

Behold! I tell you a mystery. We shall not all sleep, but we shall all be changed, in a moment, in the twinkling of an eye, at the last trumpet. For the trumpet will sound, and the dead will be raised imperishable, and we shall be changed. For this perishable body must put on the imperishable, and this mortal body must put on immortality. When the perishable puts on the imperishable, and the mortal puts on immortality, then shall come to pass the saying that is written:

> "Death is swallowed up in victory."
> "O death, where is your victory?
> O death, where is your sting?"
>
> The sting of death is sin, and the power of sin is the law. But thanks be to God, who gives us the victory through our Lord Jesus Christ.

Our future is known. It is a physical resurrection from the dead and eternal life. We confess this sure and certain confidence we have before God to the world. There is wonderful clarity and simplicity to this. A clear confession has a way of doing that. It speaks the truth like a breath of fresh air amid the smog of so many lies, false hopes, and attacks that attempt to suffocate us and God's Word.

The Formula of Concord helps show us how God's Word and the confession of His doctrine comforts us by examining election or predestination. It addresses this topic because of some controversies that were circulating at the time that were false and robbed Christians of great comfort. Even after this writing in the late 1500s, false teaching about predestination reemerged. There was a whole predestination controversy that the first president of The Lutheran Church—Missouri Synod, Walther, took part in, where Walther himself used the Formula of Concord to confess the truth of the Scriptures.

There are many points that Article XI of the Formula of Concord address, and it teaches us to look to where God is known in the Scriptures and to be careful how we speculate about matters where He has not spoken. It also shows us that in clinging to what God reveals to us in His Word, we have great consolation and comfort because we have Christ and His promises. Finally, it shows us how to think confessionally as we consider all that God says, take it to heart, and consider it.

Knowing and trusting Scripture, we confess our future is secure as the baptized people of God. The Solid Declaration confesses,

Holy Scripture also testifies that God, who has called us, is faithful. So when He has begun the good work in us, He will also preserve it to the end and perfect it, if we ourselves do not turn from Him, but firmly hold on to the work begun to the end. He has promised His grace for this very purpose. (See 1 Corinthians 1:9; Philippians 1:6; 1 Peter 5:10; 2 Peter 3:9; Hebrews 3:2.)

We should concern ourselves with this revealed will of God. We should follow and diligently think about it. Through the Word, by which He calls us, the Holy Spirit bestows grace, power, and ability for this purpose.[87]

God has called us to repentance and saving faith, and everything relies on His faithfulness and grace. Those promises define who we are and what we concern ourselves with as we face tribulation in our daily lives. We firmly hold onto the work God has done and trust that He will guard and keep us until that Last Day.

In terms of our confession, we steadfastly continue to hear and speak what God reveals to us. Thinking confessionally means speaking to others what God has spoken to us. Though a bit lengthy, we read and consider the centrality of God's Word in an excerpt from Article XI of the Solid Declaration:

This is how much of the mystery of predestination is revealed to us in God's Word. If we abide by this teaching and cling to it, it is a very useful, saving,

87 FC SD XI 32–33.

consoling teaching. It establishes very effectively the article that we are justified and saved without any works and merits of ours, purely out of grace alone, for Christ's sake. Before the time of the world, before we existed, yes, even before the foundation of the world was laid—when, of course, we could do nothing good—we were chosen by grace in Christ to salvation, according to God's purpose (Romans 9:11; 2 Timothy 1:9). Furthermore, all opinions and erroneous teachings about the powers of our natural will are overthrown by this. God in His counsel, before the time of the world, decided and ordained that He Himself would produce and work in us by His Holy Spirit's power. Through the Word, He would do everything that belongs to our conversion.

This doctrine also provides the excellent, glorious consolation that God was greatly concerned about the conversion, righteousness, and salvation of every Christian. He so faithfully <provided for it> that even before the foundation of the world was laid, He considered it, and in His purpose ordained how He would bring me to salvation and preserve me in salvation. He wanted to secure my salvation so well and so certainly, since through the weakness and wickedness of our flesh salvation could easily be lost from our hands, or through the devil's and the world's craft and might it could be snatched and taken from us. Therefore, He ordained in His eternal purpose what cannot fail or be overthrown. He placed salvation for safekeeping in the almighty hand of our Savior, Jesus Christ, from which no one can snatch us (John 10:28). Therefore, Paul asks in Romans, because we "are called according to His purpose"

(8:28), who "will be able to separate us from the love of God in Christ Jesus our Lord"? (8:39).

Furthermore, this doctrine provides glorious consolation under the cross and amid temptations. In other words, God in His counsel, before the time of the world, determined and decreed that He would assist us in all distresses. He determined to grant patience, give consolation, nourish and encourage hope, and produce an outcome for us that would contribute to our salvation. Also, Paul teaches this in a very consoling way. He explains that God in His purpose has ordained before the time of the world by what crosses and sufferings He would conform every one of His elect to the image of His Son. His cross shall and must work together for good for everyone, because they are called according to God's purpose. Therefore, Paul has concluded that it is certain and beyond doubt that neither "tribulation, or distress," neither "death nor life," or other such things "will be able to separate us from the love of God in Christ Jesus our Lord." (See Romans 8:28, 29, 35, 38, 39.)

This article provides a glorious testimony that God's Church will exist and abide in opposition to all the gates of hell [Matthew 16:18]. Likewise, it teaches what God's true Church is, so that we may not be offended by the great authority of the false church (Romans 9:24–25).[88]

The language and message of this document preaches to all of God's grace found in Christ. It roots us steadfastly in God's Word, which will not waver. Is it any wonder that this doctrine is often used

88 FC SD XI 43–50.

and proclaimed at the deathbed of Christians? As we draw our last breaths in this life, God breathes life into us through His words of consolation and peace in Christ. As we go through this life, God conforms us to the image of His Son, and nothing will separate us from the love of God in Christ Jesus, our Lord.

This is the truth, goodness, and beauty that is the Book of Concord. The eyes of the Lutheran Confessions are oriented toward the horizon, pointing Christians to the Lord Jesus, who promises He is coming again soon. They preach to us, form our confession, and even encourage us to think about the things of God in our daily lives. This is who we are as God's people and the faith that has been handed down to us through the ages. This is both the confession of the saints who have gone before and our confession, which looks with confidence to the future. Our confession in this world is always in the context of what awaits us on the Last Day, when Christ will come and we will be raised to live with Him and all His saints forever.

QUESTIONS FOR FURTHER STUDY AND DISCUSSION:

1. How does the Augsburg Confession, Article XVII, sound like the Three Ecumenical Creeds? Can something be said about the simplicity of an end-times theology found in these confessions?

2. Read the Solid Declaration of the Formula of Concord, Article IX. How does this article help form how we think about what is known and what is unknown when it comes to the Christian faith?

Conclusion

For thorough, permanent unity in the Church, it is necessary, above all things, that we have a comprehensive, unanimously approved summary and form of teaching. The common doctrine must be brought together from God's Word and reduced to a small circle of teaching, which the churches that are of the true Christian religion must confess. They must do this just as the Ancient Church always had its fixed symbols for this use.[89]

The Christian Church confesses Christ. This is who we are as God's people. The Lutheran Confession confess Christ, and we subscribe to them because they are a faithful exposition of the Word of God. Thinking confessionally, then, is really thinking scripturally.

As we have looked at various topics, we have seen how the documents of the Lutheran Confessions are used to help shape and form our confession of Christ in the world. They help us think about what God has created, who we are, who Christ is, what the church is, what the world needs, and countless other related topics. Throughout this book, we have seen how thinking about the things of God through the "normed norm" (see Introduction) of the Lutheran Confessions

89 FC SD The Comprehensive Summary, Foundation, Rule and Norm 1.

helps us proclaim Christ and the salvation He has won for us. There is great consolation in the confession made by the Book of Concord.

Likewise, we see the consolation we confess as we think about and use the Lutheran Confessions in our daily lives. We do this, too, in the long line of the church throughout the ages making the faithful confession no matter the cost. Their confession is still our confession.

What a joy it is to read through the Lutheran Confessions, think about them, and confess them. The faithful confession of Christ and His Word is of upmost importance. The confidence to confess the faith boldly is given by God Himself. May the Lord grant us all the same heart, mind, and steadfastness of these confessors so that we will continue to confess and hold fast this same faith "once delivered to the saints" (Jude 3).

APPENDIX

Overview of and Guide to the Lutheran Confessions for Study

Regularly studying the Lutheran Confessions is a beneficial habit. Various resources exist that can help us in this task. For example, *Treasury of Daily Prayer* from Concordia Publishing House provides suggested daily readings to go along with Scripture and prayer for your devotional life. Some congregations also offer weekly studies on the Lutheran Confessions or monthly reading groups. The goal in these opportunities is to be students not only of the Holy Scriptures but of the Lutheran Confessions.

What follows in this appendix is meant to be a simple overview and guide as you read through the Book of Concord and meditate upon what you are reading. The summaries provided are meant to help us in following and applying the lines of thought, important points, definitions, distinctions, and cohesiveness in each article and the whole of the Lutheran Confessions. Diving into these documents, you will see how they help form and shape your confession and your life in Christ.

Three Ecumenical Creeds

The Lutheran Confessions begin with the Three Ecumenical Creeds for a reason. The faith that is confessed in these documents is not new. It is the "catholic faith" that has been handed down by Jesus in the Holy Scriptures. The reformers are not saying anything new by including the Three Ecumenical Creeds at the beginning of the Book of Concord. Rather, the reformers confess, flowing from the Scriptures, the doctrines that have been believed, taught, and confessed by the church for centuries. The Three Ecumenical Creeds set forth the confession of biblical doctrine from the Scriptures. The very nature of the Christian faith is to confess or say back what God has revealed in His Word. This is to be done before God and men.

There are some important elements seen in the Three Ecumenical Creeds that continue throughout the Lutheran Confessions. One of these elements is the clarity and continuity of the use of specific terms. In the Apostles' Creed, the terms *Father, Son,* and *Spirit* are used in connection with the work of each person of the Trinity. The terms established in the Ecumenical Creeds are further expounded upon and confessed in the Lutheran Confessions. We also see how ambiguity is avoided in the Ecumenical Creeds. Instead, they make a clear delineation between truth and error. Confessing what the Scriptures teach necessitates including a rejection of false teaching. Everything in the Ecumenical Creeds involves confessing who God is, who He is not, and what He has accomplished for us in Christ. The Lutheran Confessions extend this pattern established in the Ecumenical Creeds by drawing clear lines between true and false teaching.

The Augsburg Confession

Articles I–XX contain some important points. The first is the clarity of the confession. Even if each of these articles is rather short, each delineates a clear confession between truth and error. Even in the condemnatory clauses, the faith is confessed. This establishes a pattern for both the Augsburg Confession and the Book of Concord.

The second thing to note is the ordering of the articles. These are laid out systematically. Take note of how this ordering correlates with how the faith is confessed. One example of this is how Article IV, the chief article, flows directly into Article V. Laying out our justification, Melanchthon then confesses how we have this saving faith.

Articles XXI–XXVI address some of the abuses and false practices of the papists. Doctrine and practice relate that what we do is a confession of what we believe, and vice versa. This is prominently seen in terms of the mass, AC XXIV. Melanchthon makes the point that the Lutheran Church doesn't "throw the baby out with the bath water," so to speak. Instead, everything is evaluated according to the Word of God. Elements of bread and wine are retained in Holy Communion, which aligns with Scripture. As was established at the beginning of the Book of Concord with the inclusion of the Three Ecumenical Creeds, the Lutheran Church is not a sect that started in the 1500s. Rather, the Lutheran Church confesses the "catholic faith," which has been handed down by Christ to the apostles up to the present. Our connection with those who have gone before us in the faith in what we both believe and do is intentional. The Lutheran Confessions seek to reject, correct, and bring stray teachings back in line with the Holy Scriptures. The Confessions lead us to a universal understanding of worship in the church that doesn't just see each person or congregation doing whatever they see fit at the time or because of the current trend.

While monasteries are a subject of Article XXVII, the broader topic discussed is serving God. God established our lives to be lived in faith toward Him and in love toward our neighbors.

The last article, XXVIII, concerns church authority. At no point does it argue for a sort of ecclesial anarchy. It clearly confesses that church and secular authority exist in this world. A great deal of what church authority is and should be comes back to what has already been stated in the Augsburg Confession concerning the church and the office of the ministry. Article XXVIII states that the authority of bishops, which is the Office of the Keys, is seen in faithfully exercising the Word of God and the Sacraments and all that comes with those duties. Likewise, we take note of this teaching and hold our church leaders to carry out the calling God has explicitly given to them.

The Apology of the Augsburg Confession

The opening articles of the Apology cover a great deal of information, but all of it centers around the proper understanding of justification. Melanchthon thoughtfully and thoroughly addresses each doctrine, defines terms, and shows how each relates to corollary topics. The Apology displays this elegant alignment well throughout its content and structure.

Article II, "Original Sin," contains an important explanation about concupiscence (as detailed in chapter 5) and how it is sin. Melanchthon addresses the false understanding of the papists and where their confession of sin leads, which relates to how one properly understands righteousness according to the Scriptures. Going from this then to Article III on Christ and then Article IV, we see the connection. Article IV of the Apology is one of the greatest confessions in the Lutheran Confessions on the doctrine of justification. It addresses with clarity Law and Gospel, the righteousness of faith, the means of grace, and so many other things. Justification is the doctrine of the Christian faith and is at the heart of the Reformation.

Article V is long and contains a great deal of content. Its discussion of love and fulfilling the Law is of utmost importance. In the case of this article, the dispute is "whether confidence is to be placed in Christ or in our works."[90] To understand the proper role of good works, then, we must know how we are justified before God. It is interesting to note that "faith alone" is written fifteen times in this article. Melanchthon makes clear that it is only through faith in Christ that man is justified before God. It is not faith plus love or works, but simply faith alone. It also addresses the importance of

90 Ap V 35.

how faith is defined, leading into what it means to live a new life in Christ. This article makes it clear that good works are required of the Christian and are a fruit of saving faith. Faith comes first, and then love follows it as a fruit. The preaching of Law and Gospel in the life of the Christian is interwoven in all of this. This discussion of justification addresses the role reason plays in the Christian life, how presuppositions must be laid aside when reading the Word of God, and the importance of letting the plain sense of the text speak for itself. Melanchthon lays out his arguments, building upon what has already been written. In his defense, point by point, he reiterates repeatedly what faith is or isn't and how Law and Gospel, rightly divided, play a role in salvation. Learning the skill of how to think theologically is another great treasure of the Apology and really the whole of the Lutheran Confessions.

Continuing, Article V, paragraphs 213–79, confesses the importance of God's mercy, which leads Melanchthon to write a great deal about it, explaining what it is and how it is connected to God's grace. The whole concept of "reward," which was used at the time by the Roman Catholics, also comes into play here. At one point, Melanchthon writes, "We are not trying to start a needless word battle about the term *reward*. But this is a great, exalted, and very important matter about where Christian hearts can find true and certain comfort."[91] Rather than simply "splitting hairs," these important distinctions are part of properly confessing and defending biblical doctrine. It is important to define the church in terms of its relationship to the means of grace, as is seen in Articles VII–XI. The focus of these articles is on what God delivers even as He has justified us in Christ rather than the governance of a man in Rome. The fact there are hypocrites within the church on earth is no fault of God nor wicked ministers. God still uses His Word and Sacraments, even if they are being preached and administered by wicked men. Melanchthon teaches on the proper place of human traditions in the church in

91 Ap V 241.

Articles VII and VIII. Though traditions are not rejected, as we have seen in prior articles, they do not merit our righteousness before God. For the sake of peace and catholicity, however, traditions are kept within the church and can be seen as good and beneficial things. The rejection of ceremonies that do not contradict the Word of God often leads to unnecessary division among the Body of Christ. Article XI, "Confession," reiterates again many of the same things we read in the Augsburg Confession. Note that the objection the papists had to that article in the Augsburg Confession was mainly that they wanted a law mandating the full enumeration of sins. The reformers rightly confess against this and view Confession and Absolution not in terms of a burden on the conscience but rather a gift for Christians to receive the absolution of Christ.

Article XII deals with repentance, an important issue in the Apology. In both the Augsburg Confession and the Apology, repentance is defined as having two parts: contrition and faith. Often, we want to view contrition as simply saying "I'm sorry." While this is not entirely wrong, look instead at how Melanchthon emphasizes the element of "terror." Hearing God's Law exposes us. It drives us to terror over our sin and the just punishment we deserve for it. The point of the contrition that terror brings, though, is how it brings about the second element of repentance: faith. Trusting solely in Christ for forgiveness, we look outside of ourselves and to His merit for us. God works through His Word. Melanchthon writes, "God's two chief works among people are these: to terrify; to justify and make alive those who have been terrified. Into these two works all Scriptures has been distributed."[92] It is interesting again to see this discussion of Law and Gospel, reinforcing the importance of how God works through His Word in all of Christian doctrine. Understanding repentance rightly goes back to understanding the proper distinction of Law and Gospel. Melanchthon further conveys the value placed on Confession and Absolution by the churches of

92 Ap XIIa 53.

the Augsburg Confession. He writes, "We also keep Confession, especially because of the Absolution. Absolution is God's Word which, by divine authority, the Power of the Keys pronounces upon individuals. Therefore, it would be wicked to remove private Absolution from the Church. If anyone despises private Absolution, he does not understand what the forgiveness of sins or the Power of the Keys is."[93]

Article XIII contains a discussion about the number and use of the Sacraments. Melanchthon makes the point that we are not dogmatic about the specific number. Rather, we see each thing for what it is according to the institution of God. The point of this article is for us to rightly use the Sacraments. Faith, not just the mere working of the Sacraments like in Roman Catholic doctrine, is required for the benefits of the Sacraments to be received. The Sacraments are joined to God's promises. Looking in faith to the means of grace, we have great consolation and comfort in Christ.

Article XIV emphasizes that by no means should Lutherans endorse having anyone and everyone preaching and administering the Sacraments. Only men who have been "rightly called" are to exercise these duties. This is because of the divine command and institution of the office of the holy ministry. Melanchthon acknowledges the scriptural teaching on the one divine office: pastor. Some other orders and offices, like bishops (other than how the Scriptures speak of this term for pastors of congregations), superintendents, and district presidents are created by human authority. Though God establishes only one rightly called office of pastor, Christians also have the freedom, so to speak, in establishing other offices to assist in church government.

The article on human traditions in the church, Article XV, is lengthy. It reiterates what was confessed in other articles. Take note, though, of Melanchthon's focus on the proper understanding of tradition within the church. There needs to be a proper understanding

93 Ap XIIb 2–4.

that avoids two ditches. We don't insist on human traditions, ordinances, and rites to merit our forgiveness, but we also don't throw out traditions that are beneficial to God's people. This is one of the great teachings the Lutheran Church has rightly understood and upheld through the centuries. Melanchthon appeals to the church fathers as they understood this use of church traditions in the same way as the reformers.

Article XVI addresses the issue of political order—another place where there is a tendency to slip to the extreme and teach that Christians cannot be involved in worldly government. The reformers clearly deny this, and we see that Christians can and do serve their neighbors in this way. The point is also made about Christian perfection through faith in Christ and not through something as ridiculous as not owning property (as was emphasized in the false teachings on the monastic life).

It is worth noting how short Article XVII is since it is about the return of Christ and the Last Day. The Scriptures teach that this is not a complicated issue. Likewise, the cause of sin, confessed in Article XIX, is also very clear, and both articles were agreed to by the Roman Catholic Church.

Article XXI in the Apology addresses the right honor of the saints and Jesus as our only mediator. The first part is seen in paragraphs 4–9 and contains three reasons why we honor saints. There is not an "anti-saint" bent to this article. Rather, it extols the saints for the right reasons. Lutherans still celebrate feasts and festivals of saints during the Church Year. Yet the whole time, Melanchthon appeals to the Scriptures for our proper understanding and practice of honoring those who have died in the faith.

The issue of both kinds in the Lord's Supper is very clear and simple. Article XXII confesses that both kinds, bread and wine, are to be given to the laity as the Words of Institution are extolled. These words of Christ inform us of our practice that Jesus plainly teaches we are to eat His body and drink His blood in the Lord's Supper. Melanchthon wrote, "The Sacrament was instituted to comfort terrified minds. This happens when they believe that Christ's flesh is given as food for the life of the world [John 6:51] and when they believe that, being joined to Christ, they are made alive."[94] Denying both kinds to the laity in the Sacrament is unbiblical and, as Melanchthon says more than once, "rude."

The issue of forced clerical celibacy in Article XXIII is also clearly against both God's Word and natural law. Melanchthon methodically lays out the argument against the command of the papists by appealing to God's Word. He first goes to the institution of marriage given by God in Genesis 1, before the fall into sin. He then moves from the creation of man and woman to what it means to desire the opposite sex in a pure way and live in the married estate. It is interesting to see how he extols both marriage and chastity, here synonymous with living a nonforced celibate life. The difference with chastity, though, is that Paul says this is a peculiar gift granted to some for the sake of the kingdom of God (see 1 Corinthians 7:7). Whether married or celibate, however, living a sexually pure life according to his station is the duty of the Christian.[95] Toward the middle of Article XXIII, beginning around paragraph 41, Melanchthon makes a connection to the doctrine of the office of the ministry. The Roman Catholic Church understanding of the priesthood attempted to draw a one-to-one comparison with the Levitical priesthood in the Old Testament, and thereby the observance of the ceremonial law. This is not the case with the pastoral office and the Old Testament Levites, as Melanchthon points out. He also shows other inconsistencies in the Roman Catholic Church thought about priesthood.

Article XXIV addresses a lot of issues, all of them related to the umbrella of "the mass" and what it entails in broad and narrow senses. Really, this article is very practical and shows us so much of what it means to go to church, why retaining certain practices are important, why it's important to rightly understand the Word

94 Ap XXII 10.

95 Ap XXIII 19.

and Sacraments, and how the mass is connected to the person and work of Christ as our only true atoning sacrifice. We do well to always keep these things in mind when we consider why and how we worship God.

Much of the discussion concerning monastic vows in Article XXVII revolves around how the self-made works of monks do away with the Gospel of Christ. This applies to the works, exercises, and disciplines they practice. In and of themselves, some of these observances aren't necessarily bad, but when the Roman Catholic Church falsely attaches saving merits to them, they become a severe problem.

Article XXVIII addresses many issues similar to the ones in the previous article. Here, though, we see the role of bishops in the church. The bishops' "dominion" is not apart from the Gospel. That is, their authority is the Word of God, which they are called to preach and teach faithfully. When bishops or other church rulers depart from the Word, they overstep their dominion.

The close of the Apology sums up well the mindset in this whole document and the confidence in the Holy Scriptures: "For now, this is our response to the Confutation. Now we leave it to the discernment of all the godly whether the adversaries are right in bragging that they have actually, from the Scriptures, refuted our Confession."[96]

Smalcald Articles

In the Preface and Parts I and II, one sees a passionate Luther who knows how important all he is confessing is. Christ is the Lord, and the doctrine of justification is the chief article. The salvation of people is at stake in these articles, and a clear confession of what Scripture teaches is a must.

Part I of the Smalcald Articles is a confession of the Trinity in a creedal-like structure. Part II is a clear confession of Christ and His work. Luther teaches justification and emphasizes its importance in

96 Ap XXVIII 26–27.

Article I. He writes, "Upon this article everything that we teach and practice depends in opposition to the pope, the devil, and the whole world. Therefore, we must be certain and not doubt this doctrine. Otherwise, all is lost, and the pope, the devil, and all adversaries win the victory and the right over us."[97]

In Part II, Article II, Luther writes, "Above and before all other popish idolatries the Mass has been the chief and most false."[98] Luther stresses an important abuse. For him to bring this up immediately after the chief article is quite telling. The connection between doctrine and practice is seen especially in the mass, where the Roman Catholic teaching undermines justification by faith alone. Read the rest of Part II, Article II, to further discover how he speaks and connects other central doctrines to the abuses of the Roman Mass.

The articles that follow in Part II also pertain to justification, as Luther lays out specific abuses. The very Gospel and Christian faith is attacked when false doctrine and practices are promoted and connected to the doctrine of justification.

Luther defines a lot of topics and terms in the Smalcald Articles, Part III, Articles III–XV. As in the Apology, this is a helpful way of confessing the faith as it delineates truth from error. This method helps teach us how to be faithful confessors of the faith in our day as well. We don't have to be theologians on the scale of Luther to make great confessions of the faith. We simply have to speak what Scripture teaches. The Smalcald Articles aid in our task in helping us speak in a clear and faithful way.

The doctrine of justification runs through all the remaining articles of Part III. Article III, "Repentance," defines true repentance versus false repentance. The issue of concupiscence and how it is connected to a proper repentance and the forgiveness of Christ is brought up again. Articles IV–VIII provide some great teachings on the means of grace. Luther speaks of how God delivers the Gospel

97 SA II I 5.

98 SA II II 1.

to us through the Word and Sacraments and what consolation we have in them. Article VIII, "Confession," speaks about this topic, to be sure, but Luther also goes into a discussion about how the Holy Spirit works through the Word and Sacraments, warning us against seeking God elsewhere. "Therefore, we must constantly maintain this point: God does not want to deal with us in any other way than through the spoken Word and the Sacraments. Whatever is praised as the Spirit—without the Word and Sacraments—is the devil himself."[99]

Treatise on the Power and Primacy of the Pope

This work by Melanchthon is sometimes seen as an addendum to the Smalcald Articles and was originally meant to be attached to the end of the Augsburg Confession. But it really is best seen as its own document. Reading this document is quite easy in the sense that the refutations and arguments are laid out in an extremely organized way. Each section is presented in a systematic manner that defends the point being made. It really is quite a model for the church to see how Melanchthon writes, as well as his theological method starting with Scripture and then using other sources such as councils and church fathers who attest to what the Bible teaches.

The first section deals with the office of the papacy and how this office is against the Gospel. The claims made by the pope not only go against the Scriptures but church history. It's interesting to see how Melanchthon points out instances when previous popes made statements against what would later be codified as canon law. This shows the sinister nature of the papacy and how it fulfills the scriptural prophecies of the antichrist. We are wise to be aware of and avoid the papacy even to this day.

The final section is a very practical confession of the office of the ministry in relation to the church. Notice how Melanchthon speaks here about the proper duties of the pastoral office and what the

99 SA III VIII 10.

church possesses by divine right in calling and ordaining ministers. While there may be some distinctions in offices within the church by human authority, there is only one office by divine authority, the pastoral office. The doctrine of the church, which includes both pastors and laity, is important. It's a great thing to understand all of this properly as this is what the Scriptures teach. We rejoice in the order of God as He has given us His church, where Christ and His benefits are found and given out in the means of grace.

The Small and Large Catechisms

Though they are placed later in the Book of Concord, after the Creeds, Luther's Large and Small Catechisms are the next chronological documents. The prefaces lay before the reader the heart of Luther as a pastor and doctor of the church. In the catechisms, the language of Scripture is overflowing. Even if direct quotes are not referenced, biblical language permeates each chief part. Not only are we instructed about Christian doctrine in these works, but we also can learn how to speak about the things of God using the language of Scripture.

The Longer Preface of the Large Catechism is directed primarily toward pastors who refuse to teach and preach the Large Catechism (the Christian faith). Pastors should keep this admonishment in mind as to their duty as ministers of God. Like in the Small Catechism, the situation in the churches is mentioned in the Preface. Luther then turns his attention to fathers in the Short Preface, specifically what is befitting to a Christian father who is called to also teach the faith at home as the head of his household. Preachers and hearers do well to listen to the words of Luther in these prefaces so we can take our Christian duty to teach and confess the faith seriously.

Luther lays out the purpose of the Commandments in Part I of the Large Catechism. There is a negative and positive sense to each commandment. The negative is a prohibition of sinful behavior, showing how we stand accused in our sins. In this way, we can see the Commandments as a confessional mirror in which we examine our lives with God's eternal and righteous Law. We also see the positive, in that our new man in Christ, created and sustained by the Gospel, desires to live in accordance with the Ten Commandments. We see what a God-pleasing life through the lens of God's Law is.

The first two commandments teach us about a proper fear, love, and trust in the true God over and above everything else that we turn into idols. Connected to them is God's holy name. A good and faithful confession of the Scriptures honors God's name, whereas false doctrine and teaching are a great sin against the Second Commandment. In all, the same Lord who is the true God has placed His holy name upon us, and we confess that name as we faithfully confess His Word.

Luther provides some helpful background to the Third Commandment. He explains the Sabbath in terms of the ceremonial law of the Old Testament and how we are to understand this commandment today. He emphasizes the importance and holiness inherent in God's Word. We are made holy by God, and we are to hold His Word as a treasure. As Christians, this is what the Third Commandment is about: hearing and learning God's Word. Luther also conveys the importance of setting time aside for participating in the Divine Service. God's people are made holy by the Word of God, and they gather together to hear and learn the Word preached to them. This leads to another point; Luther urges the intentional retention of what has been handed down to us. Sunday is the day Christians gathered from the beginning of the church, and Luther encourages that this should still be the case. The Lutheran Church is not a sect but a continuation of the catholic faith, the same faith confessed in the Three Ecumenical Creeds. Scripture is the only authority, but that does not mean we don't value the traditions and customs that have been handed down to us by our forefathers in the faith. Holding God's Word in this high regard, Luther states, "For this reason, particular places, times, persons, and the entire outward order of worship have been created and appointed, so that there may be order in public practice [1 Corinthians 14:40]."[100] Perhaps the best summary of the discussion of the Third Commandment can be seen toward the end in paragraph 100. Luther teaches us, "Therefore, you must always have God's Word in your heart, upon your lips, and in your ears."[101]

The Fourth Commandment, a long section of the Large Catechism, introduces the second table of the Law. God teaches us how we are to relate to our neighbor. God has established fathers and mothers as a special office within His creation. "To the position of fatherhood and motherhood God has given special distinction above all positions that are beneath it: He does not simply command us to love our parents, but to honor them."[102] In all these things, the Lord's order is designed for our good. We are called to honor our father and mother, just as parents are called to raise their children in the Christian faith.

The Fifth Commandment continues to draw Christians outside of themselves. It commands us to consider our neighbor and his well-being. God works to protect people through this commandment. Luther states in paragraph 183, "God well knows that the world is evil [Galatians 1:4], and that this life has much unhappiness. Therefore, He has set up this and the other commandments between the good people and the evil."[103] The call of Christians is to not harm their neighbors but to protect and defend them. This is another example of Luther teaching how God both prohibits and instructs us in the Commandments. This is further explained at the end of this commandment's section (paragraphs 196–98), where Luther shows how God teaches us in His Word what are true good works and what a new holy life in Christ looks like.

In paragraph 200 on the Sixth Commandment, Luther addresses the neighbor personally: "Then they proceed to talk about the person

100 LC I 94.

101 LC I 100.

102 LC I 105.

103 LC I 183.

nearest him, or the closest possession next after his body, namely, his wife. She is one flesh and blood with him [Genesis 2:23–24], so that we cannot inflict a higher injury upon him in any good that is his."[104] Luther explains marriage in both estates: even though it relates to the civil realm, marriage should be defined by God's Word. Marriage is to be regarded not only highly but as necessary.

The Seventh Commandment concerns itself with temporal property. It is far reaching in its scope. Like the Fifth Commandment, here there is a command to do no harm to our neighbor as well as a teaching for us to help our neighbor protect his property and possessions. The attitude of the Christian is to be one of service and not of self-promotion.

The Eighth Commandment speaks of honor and good reputation. A lot of confusion surrounds how this commandment is to be lived out. Luther, however, provides a clear biblical explanation that we should hear and follow. It's worth noting how Luther forms the scope of this commandment beginning in paragraph 260 before moving on in 262 and 263. An important question to ask regarding this commandment is "Has God given me the office to speak in this matter?" When we are called to speak, we are to faithfully speak the truth in love.

The Ninth and Tenth Commandments reveal our sinful impulses to have a higher status and possess more than others. God humbles us, however, and reveals our hearts. Even if something may appear "right" in the eyes of the world, the Lord knows our covetous and deceitful intentions, even if we do not always act upon them. Luther concludes by saying, "So this commandment will remain, like all the rest, one that will constantly accuse us and show how godly we are in God's sight!"[105]

"The Conclusion of the Ten Commandments" helps us understand how we should view God's Law as Christians. God lays before us what

---

104 LC I 200.

105 LC I 310.

is good and pleasing to Him. As we study these Commandments and as they are preached to us by our pastors, God's Law indeed accuses us. So long as we are in the world and our old sinful nature still hangs around our necks, the Law will always do that. At no point in the Large Catechism is there any talk or indication that our salvation is accomplished by the Law.

There is a problem, however, when we view the Law in a negative light. God's Law is indeed good, as Luther has taught throughout the Ten Commandments. As Christians live their new lives in Christ, given and worked by the Gospel, they are taught by God's Law. Through the Law, the Lord lays before His people the instruction of what is a godly life and what works are pleasing in His sight. Though Christians are still sinners and the old man of our sinful natures will always be accused by the Law, the new man of our new life in Christ worked by the Gospel delights in God's Law as the guide to bear the fruit of faith.

Living in all three estates (church, family, and secular), Christians occupy themselves with the Ten Commandments and what they teach. Luther states, "Just occupy yourself with them. Try your best. Apply all power and ability. You will find so much to do that you will neither seek nor value any other work or holiness."[106] Christians don't create for themselves new works to be done, for God has already placed these works before them in the Commandments. As we live our new lives in Christ, good works flow from our faith in God our Father.

Moving from the Ten Commandments in the Large Catechism to the Apostles' Creed, we see a confession of who God is as Father, Son, and Holy Spirit. Luther states, "So the Creed is nothing other than the answer and confession of Christians arranged with respect to the First Commandment."[107] We confess in how each person of the Trinity works both in His distinct person and with respect to

106 LC I 318.

107 LC II 10.

the other persons of the Trinity in the unity of the Godhead. The Second Article is the hinge of the Creed, as the First points to it and the Third points back to and flows from it. Understanding Jesus as Lord goes hand in hand with who He is as the Redeemer and the doctrine of the atonement. It is a bit surprising that this section on the Second Article is so short, yet it is packed with such beauty and comfort.

Luther begins his discussion of the Third Article by stating, "I cannot connect this article (as I have said) to anything better than Sanctification. Through this article the Holy Spirit, with His office, is declared and shown: He makes people holy [1 Corinthians 6:11]."[108] Normally we would associate sanctification in terms of the Christian life of a new obedience and good works (See, for example, AC VI and FC SD IV), yet Luther here seems to connect this article with the previous article. The primary focus of the Third Article of the Creed, here in the Large Catechism, is the distribution of salvation accomplished by Jesus on the cross. This is why Luther uses sanctification in a broader sense. An important part of this article is the location of the means of grace within the church. Pastors often hear, "I don't need to go to church to be a Christian," but the Large Catechism, teaching what Scripture teaches, says something quite different. The Holy Spirit works through the Word and Sacraments. We don't go searching for the Holy Spirit anywhere else. It is in and through the means of grace that God gives us Christ and His benefits. Luther clearly warns against separating oneself from the church; it is a grave matter because it separates one from God.

The three articles of the Creed specifically confess who our triune God is and what He does. Confessing the Creed rings forth the truth of God and separates us from all false gods and religions. It also shows us what God has done, as opposed to what God demands, as we saw in the Ten Commandments. In a concluding thought to this second part of the Large Catechism, Luther writes, "Here we

108 LC III 35.

see that God gives Himself to us completely. He gives all that He has and is able to do in order to aid and direct us in keeping the Ten Commandments. The Father gives all creatures. The Son gives His entire work. And the Holy Spirit bestows all His gifts."[109]

Luther begins the discussion on the Lord's Prayer in the Large Catechism with a general theology of prayer. In a brief definition, Luther states, "To call upon God's name is nothing other than to pray."[110] Prayer is directed to God and connected to the right use of the name of God as we see in the Second Commandment. The language of Father and child is found throughout this section as we explore what it means to call upon God in prayer. We are God's children who ask and receive from our gracious Father even something so basic as our daily bread. Prayer is a serious matter and is formed by God's Word. God listens and answers our petitions and forms and shapes our reverence to Him.

The sermonic nature of the Large Catechism is evident here as Luther's word choice addresses us as hearers of the Word of God. Notice the back and forth and proper distinction between Law and Gospel throughout this section on the Lord's Prayer. It is a humbling thing to pray these petitions. As we do, we look outside of ourselves and see that our only help is found in the One who hears and answers us as only He can. Finally, Luther keeps pointing us back to the Scriptures, where God speaks to us and shows us how the things we pray for are fulfilled and answered in Christ.

It is interesting to note how Luther begins the discussion of the Fifth Petition by saying, "This part now applies to our poor miserable life. Although we have and believe God's Word, do, and submit to His will, and are supported by His gifts and blessings, our life is still not sinless. We still stumble daily and transgress because we live in the world among people."[111] We know all too well that we sin

109 LC II 69.

110 LC III 5.

111 LC III 86.

against our neighbor and our neighbor sins against us. This stresses the reality that we daily need to pray to God and call upon Him for mercy. Asking God to not hold our sin against us is to pray in faith, trusting in the person and work of Christ as our mediator. Knowing how we stand before the Father on account of the Son gives us confidence in our daily lives.

In the Sixth Petition, we pray against our fallen flesh, the world, and the devil, which seek to drive us away from God. As Christians, we have the deliverance from these things in Christ, who perfectly obeyed the Law of God and overcame the assaults of the devil. As Christians, we are armed against these fallen powers and pray that we would not fall away but ultimately have the victory. We run to and take hold of God's Word and pray the Lord's Prayer for deliverance amid the temptations in this life. The Seventh Petition extends from the Sixth as it focuses specifically on the assaults of the devil. Praying this petition, we live out God's desire for us to run to Him and seek His help. We have our help in Him alone.

That little word *Amen* at the end of the Lord's Prayer contains so much. Our faith trusts the promises that God will hear and answer our petitions on account of Christ. We do not doubt but know with certainty that the Lord doesn't close His ears to our cries. Instead, as our dear Father, He listens and gives out of His grace. Like all prayers to God, the Lord's Prayer is rooted in the wonderful promises of the Gospel that we are not to despise. Instead, we gladly send our prayers before God as sweet incense rising to His throne.

Regarding Baptism, Luther first lays out where our starting point should be: Matthew 28. This way of understanding Baptism, first with Christ's institution and then spiraling out to other Scripture passages, is a significant way of understanding the theology that avoids a great deal of errors from the beginning. It takes Jesus' words seriously, as He gave such a gift to the church, as well as Scripture, which teaches and supports this doctrine.

Luther states that Baptism is no different than the Gospel itself. Baptism and the Word are not in opposition to each other.

"For indeed, the entire Gospel is an outward, verbal preaching [Romans 10:17; 1 Corinthians 1:21]. In short, what God does and works in us He intends to work through such outward ordinances. Therefore, wherever He speaks—indeed, no matter what direction or by whatever means He speaks—faith must look there. It must hold to that object."[112] Faith is not intended for faith's sake; it must have an object. The object of faith is Christ, and we apprehend Christ through the means of grace. This is why clinging to our Baptisms is nothing other than clinging to Christ. We daily cling to our Baptisms and live out our lives in repentance and faith.

The last part of the Large Catechism contains a great deal regarding the Lord's Supper and our Christian life. As with Baptism, Luther begins with Jesus' institution to establish the essence of the Sacrament and then moves to its benefits and right reception. Luther confesses that the Lord's Supper is a serious matter. He elaborates further on how we receive the true body and blood of Christ in this Sacrament in the Smalcald Articles. The reason why Luther's confession about the Lord's Supper is so clear and specific is because God's Word is clear on this matter. We take Jesus at His word and know that what God says is true. He does not lie. His Word does not err. The benefits of the Lord's Supper are wonderful. We treasure this Sacrament given to us by our Lord. Luther spends a great deal of this article admonishing and encouraging us. This is another instance where we see sections of Luther's catechetical sermons used in the Large Catechism. It's important that Luther, as a preacher, admonishes us to see the serious matter of receiving the Lord's Supper rightly and often. Yet he extols the Sacrament's gifts, encouraging us to run to it for our consolation and comfort.

The Formula of Concord

From its beginning, the Epitome of the Formula of Concord's method and style is straightforward. Each topic presents the status

112 LC IV 30–31.

of the controversy followed by affirmative and negative statements. This format carries on in the Solid Declaration, but the Epitome is written more like an outline. Such organization is helpful since these articles have implications for the people of God. This makes the Formula of Concord, in both documents, so clear in how doctrine is to be addressed and seen as practical.

The Solid Declaration emphasizes both how the Holy Scriptures are important and how they are to be regarded. In numerous places, it clearly confesses that these are the "only true standard or norm by which all teachers and doctrines are to be judged."[113] In understanding Christian doctrine, there is no doubt about the place and role of Scripture. Scripture is not simply the highest authority, as if there are other authorities or sources of doctrine. No, everything in doctrine is judged according to the Word of God alone.

Stemming from this, the Solid Declaration emphasizes how the other confessional documents are normed by the Scriptures. They are shown to confess what Scripture teaches and what has been held up in the church. In this way, it is correct to say that when someone rejects the Lutheran Confessions, he is rejecting the truth of Scripture because the Confessions confess what Scripture teaches. The language and purpose of subscribing to the confessional documents is seen here too. There is a need for the whole church to confess the same truths together. The Lutheran Confessions square our doctrine and practice because they confess what Scripture teaches. "They show what he should regard and receive as right and true according to God's Word of the prophetic and apostolic Scriptures. They also show what he should reject, shun, and avoid as false and wrong."[114]

Article I of the Solid Declaration says, "This controversy about original sin is not unnecessary wrangling. If this doctrine is rightly presented from, and according to, God's Word, and separated from all Pelagian and Manichaean errors, then the benefits of the Lord

113 FC SD Comprehensive Summary, Foundation, Rule, and Norm 3.

114 FC SD Comprehensive Summary, Foundation, Rule, and Norm 16.

Christ and His precious merit, also the gracious work of the Holy Spirit, are better known and praised even more (as the Apology says)."[115] This statement keeps us focused on the purpose of rightly understanding original sin and how God is not the creator of sin. This matters because when error is taught and promoted, Christ and His work are obscured.

Article II of the Solid Declaration contains an important discussion about free will. Much of this has been addressed already in the Augsburg Confession as referenced in paragraph 5. Note the similar language that is used with the Apology of the Augsburg Confession and where clarifications are made along with the reasons why they are made. The controversy over human will and powers wasn't just something between the Lutherans and the Roman Catholics but even within the Lutheran Church itself.

Further, Article II emphasizes the absolute mercy and working of God in our salvation. Our faith is completely the work of God through His means of grace (see especially paragraph 50). This divine working of God is a great comfort for us because it places salvation entirely in God's hands and doesn't leave our eternal salvation either up for grabs or up to us. This doctrine of the proper place of the will is integrally connected to how we understand the grace of God. This is very relevant for Lutherans, especially as we see decision theology so prevalent in the United States. Confessing who we are as sinners and our fallen will, we then rightly understand the total work of God in saving us and giving us faith in Christ as a gift, not because of our will or choice.

Paragraph 57 contains a warning against those who would not listen to the Word of God, as well as the serious consequences of this. This leads into how our will, before conversion, is worse than a stone or a block because we resist God. This is an important point to emphasize again: we are against God until we are converted by the Holy Spirit.

115 FC SD I 3.

Paragraph 63 begins the important discussion about the will of humans after they have been converted to saving faith. To summarize, we see these five points:

1. After conversion, humans want to do what is good and will delight in God's Law.
2. The Holy Spirit produces good works.
3. These good works are produced spontaneously.
4. Christians cooperate with the Holy Spirit in their new lives.
5. The Holy Spirit rules, guides, and leads Christians in their new lives.

All of these things exist in a Christian's new life. This life is drastically different from those who have not been converted. "There is a great difference between baptized and unbaptized people."[116] The Christian has been renewed. This doesn't mean that his old Adam is gone in this life, however, for the old sinful self still hangs around his neck until Christ calls him to glory. Still, we err when we forget the fact that Christians are new people and different from those who have not been converted.

Article III is a great explanation about what the righteousness of faith means. It clearly shows that faith is not some quality in us but instead it apprehends Christ and His benefits. Paragraphs 13–14 summarize why faith justifies: "Faith justifies not because it is such a good work or because it is so beautiful a virtue. It justifies because it lays hold of and accepts Christ's merit in the promise of the Holy Gospel. For this merit must be applied and become ours through faith, if we are to be justified by it. Therefore, the righteousness that is credited to faith or to the believer out of pure grace is Christ's obedience, suffering, and resurrection, since He has made satisfaction for us to the Law and paid for <expiated> our sins."[117] Article III clearly emphasizes that we have the righteousness of Christ through faith alone, which is received in the Gospel promise. There are indeed fruits

116 FC SD II 67.

117 FC SD III 13–14.

of this faith, but sanctification follows justification. The confidence of the Christian rests solely in Christ. While repetitive in the Solid Declaration, this recurring theme shows the nature of faith looking outward and not within us. Note again how the closing section of this article helps define terms. A great deal of theology is clarified when key words are defined and related to one another.

Article IV begins with a clear affirmation that God commands good works. We should remember this, especially as we see the doctrine of good works downplayed around us on many fronts. Though works are not the basis for our salvation, the doctrine of justification by faith alone does not do away with the command of God for us to serve our neighbors. We see instead the proper place and role of good works and how sanctification rightly flows from saving faith.

Much has been written about Law and Gospel, especially about the third use of the Law. Article V lays out the background and foundation for what is addressed in Article VI. One of the main issues addressed in Article V is the proper distinction between the Law and the Gospel, including the danger when only one of these doctrines is preached to the exclusion of the other. The preaching of both, rightly divided, is clearly upheld here by the writers.

Article VI begins by laying out how the Law of God is useful and good. Throughout this section, there is a clear confession that the Law of God is good. Likewise, see how the writers clearly explain the Law as the revealed will of God. The whole "problem" with the Law lies not in God's good Law itself but in sinful man failing to live up to it.

An important subtopic in this article is man as *simul iustus et peccator* (simultaneously justified and a sinner). The Law, then, is seen for both the old man and the new man. The accusations of the Law rightly accuse and kill the old Adam. The Christian man, the new Adam, however, does not live under the Law but now has a new life in Christ because of the Gospel. He no longer lives under the

Law, but he lives in the Law. This means that he delights in what God's Law says and teaches him.

Understanding that the justified man still has the old man in this life, for the Christian God's Law guides and instructs him in the new life in Christ. "The Holy Spirit uses the Law in order to teach the regenerate from it and to point out and show them in the Ten Commandments what is the 'will of God, what is <good and> acceptable and perfect' (Romans 12:2) in what 'good works, which God prepared beforehand, that we should walk' (Ephesians 2:10)."[118] The Law of God lays out what is good, right, and true for the new man to follow in his new life created by the Gospel.

Article VII, which covers the Lord's Supper, is quite lengthy because so many issues pertaining to the person and work of Christ are addressed in this doctrine. The Solid Declaration brings up the critical fact that the body and blood of Christ are received by anyone who partakes of the Lord's Supper. Only in faith are the benefits of Jesus received, while unbelievers eat and drink to their judgment. Another important aspect of this article is the term *sacramental union*, which addresses the presence of Jesus in this Sacrament. This doctrine is connected to understanding Christ and His person as fully God and fully man. All in all, this is a very straightforward article that helps us clarify and faithfully confess what this Sacrament is according to the institution of Christ as revealed in His Holy Word.

Article VIII, pertaining to the doctrine of Christ, is a good example of how understanding false views helps us clarify what is the truth. The personal union of the two natures of Christ is hard for us to grasp. When we see the teaching of Scripture confessed over and above error, however, we rightly know Jesus as fully God and fully man. This also goes with the communion, or communication, between the two natures of Christ. As high and lofty as this discussion may be, the article does an excellent job of showing the

118 FC SD VI 12.

practicality of the doctrine of Christ. One sees how this is conveyed in Article VIII with its countless ties to various doctrines.

Article X helps us understand the correct definition and use of *adiaphora*. These are not simply "indifferent" things, as if they didn't matter, but "middle things." This article mostly pertains to worship practices, but the discussion extends beyond that. We see again how actions, what we do or don't do, all confess something. Traditions have their place, and we should understand them properly. We also should be careful before we throw down or away a tradition without due cause or reason. An interesting point from the Solid Declaration is how, in a state of confusion, something that may have previously been considered to be an adiaphoron can cease to be considered as such.

Article XI contains a lot, but one thing of note is in paragraph 12: "All Scripture is inspired by God."[119] Laying out this truth is important as this article asserts that we do not go beyond what God's Word says. The purpose of this article is seen at the end of paragraph 12 through the end of paragraph 14. Understanding this properly, Article XI comforts us as it says so much about the grace of God toward us in Christ, even before the foundation of the world.

The Conclusion of the Solid Declaration gives great comfort and encouragement to the church. A critical part of the Solid Declaration, and a fitting conclusion to this book, is as follows: "In the sight of God and of all Christendom <the entire Church of Christ>, we want to testify to those now living and those who will come after us. This declaration presented here about all the controverted articles mentioned and explained above—and no other—is our faith, doctrine, and confession. By God's grace, with intrepid hearts, we are willing to appear before the judgment seat of Christ with this Confession and give an account of it [1 Peter 4:5]. We will not speak or write anything contrary to this Confession, either publicly or privately. By the strength of God's grace we intend to abide by it. Therefore,

119 FC SD XI 12.

after mature deliberation, we have, in the fear of God and by calling on His name, attached our signatures with our own hands."[120]

120 FC SD Conclusion 40.